Style and Emotion in Comic Novels and Short Stories

Also available from Bloomsbury

Corpus Stylistics in Heart of Darkness and its Italian Translations,
by Lorenzo Mastropierro
Crime Fiction Migration, by Christiana Gregoriou
Mind Style and Cognitive Grammar, by Louise Nuttall
Stylistic Manipulation of the Reader in Contemporary Fiction,
edited by Sandrine Sorlin

Style and Emotion in Comic Novels and Short Stories

Agnes Marszalek

BLOOMSBURY ACADEMIC
LONDON • NEW YORK • OXFORD • NEW DELHI • SYDNEY

BLOOMSBURY ACADEMIC
Bloomsbury Publishing Plc
50 Bedford Square, London, WC1B 3DP, UK
1385 Broadway, New York, NY 10018, USA
29 Earlsfort Terrace, DUblin 2, Ireland

BLOOMSBURY, BLOOMSBURY ACADEMIC and the Diana logo
are trademarks of Bloomsbury Publishing Plc

First published in Great Britain 2020
Paperback edition published 2021

Copyright © Agnes Marszalek, 2020

Agnes Marszalek has asserted her right under the Copyright, Designs and Patents Act, 1988, to be identified as Author of this work.

For legal purposes the Acknowledgements on p. ix constitute an extension of this copyright page.

Cover design: Ben Anslow
Cover image: Marta Marszałek

All rights reserved. No part of this publication may be reproduced or transmitted in any form or by any means, electronic or mechanical, including photocopying, recording, or any information storage or retrieval system, without prior permission in writing from the publishers.

Bloomsbury Publishing Plc does not have any control over, or responsibility for, any third-party websites referred to or in this book. All internet addresses given in this book were correct at the time of going to press. The author and publisher regret any inconvenience caused if addresses have changed or sites have ceased to exist, but can accept no responsibility for any such changes.

A catalogue record for this book is available from the British Library.

A catalog record for this book is available from the Library of Congress.

ISBN: HB: 978-1-3500-5458-5
PB: 978-1-3502-8398-5
ePDF: 978-1-3500-5459-2
eBook: 978-1-3500-5460-8

Typeset by Deanta Global Publishing Services, Chennai, India

To find out more about our authors and books visit www.bloomsbury.com and sign up for our newsletters.

Dla mojej rodziny.

Contents

List of tables		viii
Acknowledgements		ix
1	Introduction	1
2	Narrative worlds, literary emotion and humorous discourse	15
3	Experiencing modes and moods	27
4	Engaging with characters	71
5	Reacting to story structures	113
6	Conclusion	145
Notes		153
References		154
Index		166

Tables

1	Stabilizing and destabilizing cues in comic narratives	7
2	Cues, techniques and effects	148

Acknowledgements

This book is based on a doctoral thesis completed in the English Language and Linguistics subject area at the University of Glasgow and, as such, it has been shaped by the expertise and enthusiasm of the academics working there. Above all, I would like to thank my primary PhD supervisor, Cathy Emmott, whose knowledge and commitment not only have supported me throughout the process of writing the thesis, but have influenced my research ever since I was an undergraduate student. I am also grateful to Wendy Anderson and Marc Alexander, whose good advice (academic and other) has assisted me along the way. More recently, I have benefitted from the backing of my colleagues at Glasgow International College, and I would like to thank them for allowing me the flexibility to combine teaching and writing.

This study, and my research more generally, has been influenced by the work done by the members of the Poetics and Linguistics Association (PALA). I would like to express my gratitude to Michael Burke, Joanna Gavins, Ernestine Lahey, Dan McIntyre, Paul Simpson and Peter Stockwell for their feedback on the chapters, presentations and dissertations which have informed this work. Among those whose advice and support have been particularly helpful are Matt Evans, Jane Lugea, Clara Neary, Louise Nuttall, Stephen Pihlaja, Helen Ringrow, Lizzie Stewart-Shaw and Sara Whiteley. Finally, special thanks go to Marta Dynel, the editor of my first publication on humour, and Zsófia Demjén, former PI and current friend.

Of the fellow graduates of the University of Glasgow, I am particularly grateful to Nina Enemark, Anna Fisk, Kirsten Somerville, Vanessa Zidros, Robin Davis, Ryan Vance and Alex Winn for their continuing friendship, guidance and support. This book is for you.

1

Introduction

Comic novels and short stories are designed to evoke a range of affective responses. While many of these responses are primarily related to the creation of humour, some can be linked, more generally, to entertaining the reader. Much of comedy's potential to entertain is encoded in the stylistic layer of the writing, meaning that it is the language of the text which guides us to react in certain ways. A comic narrative, therefore, can be seen as a kind of linguistic manipulation which relies on specific stylistic devices that direct our emotional experience in order to entertain us.

This book explores how the language of comic novels and short stories can shape our emotional reactions in the process of reading. The focus here is on a particular aspect of the experience of written comic narratives – one which stems from texts' ability to encourage their readers to use the words on the page to create *narrative worlds*, which are imaginary spaces built partly from the linguistic elements present in the text and partly from the readers' own knowledge and cognitive mechanisms (e.g. Ryan 1980; Emmott 1997; Werth 1999). When I discuss the experience of narrative comedy, I am therefore referring to the experience of being in an alternative universe which comes into existence in the process of reading (e.g. Gerrig 1993). This universe is occupied by people, locations, objects and events – features which can evoke emotional reactions that are dependent, partly, on the ways in which these elements are linguistically represented in the text. Textual worlds are linguistically constructed: they are composed from stylistic building blocks which shape the reader's emotional experience of being in those worlds.

Although I concentrate specifically on the language of comic novels and short stories, this is not strictly a study on the creation of humour in written narratives (cf. Attardo 2001; Ermida 2008). I do, of course, discuss humour throughout, and – as expected in a stylistic account of humorous discourse (see Simpson 2006) – outline the humorous incongruities which underlie the various amusing passages I analyse. However, rather than investigating the semantic and pragmatic mechanisms involved in the creation of verbal humour (as it is done by, for example, Raskin 1985 and Attardo and Raskin 1991), I approach humour not in and of itself, but as a vehicle for the construction of the wider narrative world of the comic text. Individual instances of humour present in texts will be seen as components of such worlds, and consequently as building blocks of narrative comedy. It is comedy, not humour, which is of primary importance here, and for that reason this book draws from a range of disciplines which are well-equipped to deal with describing the structural characteristics of a long, complex comic narrative like a novel or a short story. The definition of narrative comedy adopted here is, therefore, based on research in literary, film and television studies (Frye 1957; Neale and Krutnik 1990), and it centres around three main features of comic narratives which distinguish them from those which are non-comic:

1. a prevailing comic mood,
2. a cast of comic characters, and
3. a series of comic events followed by a comic resolution.

In the chapters that follow, each of these components will be discussed from a predominantly stylistic perspective, but with references to studies of literary and film/television comedy. While the text analysis is linguistic, the overall approach adopted here is interdisciplinary.

One way to approach narrative humour is to view it not in isolation, but as part of the larger linguistic context in which it occurs – shaped and influenced by the narrative world to which it belongs. It is the construction of this world which will affect our experience of humour in the narrative. While much of our engagement with comedy does rely on the emotion of amusement evoked as a response to the humorous elements in the text, comic narratives are also designed to trigger a range of other affective reactions which are unrelated to humour, but which stem, more generally, from our involvement with the narrative world. This kind of emotional involvement with text-based characters, events and other features is associated with what psychologists refer to as our *immersion* in the world of the text which can result from the impression of being *transported* there in the course of reading (e.g. Green and Brock 2000; Green 2010, see also Miall 2007; Oatley 2011). A comic narrative may be designed to make us laugh, but it also encourages us to immerse ourselves in its world. This can involve forming feelings about the characters who inhabit it and about the events which happen to them.

Many of these feelings, in fact, can seem very far removed from the pleasurable emotional reactions typically associated with humour. While many stylistic world-building elements found in comic narratives are used for a humorous effect, some allow humour to coexist with other, sometimes painful or uncomfortable responses to narrative worlds. Rather than approaching comedy as a homogenous genre whose main purpose it is to amuse, it may be better to view it as a *mode* (see King 2002, 2011) that can be blended with other modes to evoke emotional reactions more complex than straightforward amusement. One of the novels which inform this study, Mark Haddon's *A Spot of Bother*, is a narrative which frequently uses humour in combination with elements that are distinctly non-humorous, as illustrated by the following passage:

Example 1
Jamie was kneeling on the stairs with a washing-up bowl of soapy water, sponging his father's blood from the carpet.
    That was the problem with books and films. When the big stuff happened there was orchestral music and everyone knew where to get a tourniquet and there was never an ice-cream van going by outside. Then the big stuff happened in real life and your knees hurt and the J-cloth was disintegrating in your hands and it was obvious there was going to be some kind of permanent stain.
(Haddon 2007: 293)

This extract is constructed around a tension between features which are humorous and those that are distinctly non-humorous. While it is partly the contrast between the serious 'big stuff' such as a family member's grievous injury, and the trivial, prosaic reality of ice-cream vans and J-cloths which informs the humour here, it would be a mistake to treat the passage as entirely humorous – after all, it concerns a tragic event in someone's life. The event and the person may be fictional and confined to the narrative world of the text, but it is a world in which we are immersed in the process of reading, and consequently, a world in which we may be emotionally involved. Our feelings for the character and our appraisal of the seriousness of the situation in which he finds himself, for example, are likely to affect our experience of reading the extract above, influencing our impression of humour not only in the short passage, but also in the whole novel. It is this mix of positive and negative emotion evoked in the process of reading which, for some readers, may contribute to the enjoyment of engaging with comic texts, as seen in this extract from one reader's review of *A Spot of Bother* written for the online reading community Goodreads[1]:

> [...] tender, sweet and heartbreaking. it's also hilariously funny. haddon does heartbreaking and funny with such grace, simplicity, and verbal virtuosity, it's wonderful.

Behind what the reader refers to as 'verbal virtuosity' are particular stylistic choices which allow the writer to 'do heartbreaking and funny', that is, to evoke seemingly contradictory blends of emotion. While not every narrative comedy deals with heartbreak in the way that Haddon's novel does, many do rely on our immersion in the narrative world to trigger certain responses which contribute to our experience of these worlds.

1.1. Experiencing humorous worlds

Much of the humour which appears in comic novels and short stories tends to be very context-dependent. A passage which makes us laugh in the course of reading a humorous novel, for example, may not be equally amusing when taken out of that linguistic context and presented to someone unfamiliar with the text. This familiarity is important, as comic narratives rely on their readers to accumulate certain knowledge about the narrative worlds which they present to us, and then encourage us to draw on that knowledge to identify and comprehend instances of humour. Unlike simple puns or canned jokes, which can be effective regardless of the linguistic context in which we encounter them, the humorous elements found in more complex narratives may not even be recognized as amusing by those receivers who lack the essential background knowledge of the wider text. That is because while the comprehension of puns and jokes often depends on our general knowledge of the real world, our understanding of the humour in narratives will often rely on our familiarity with the particular narrative world of the text (see Emmott 1997: 35 for *text-specific knowledge*).

Since it is the knowledge of the textual world which can influence whether we find a particular line amusing or not while reading a comic narrative, the stylistic construction of that world will, to some extent, determine the reader's experience of narrative humour. One explanation for why narrative humour can lose its amusing potential when taken out of its immediate context is that we depend on certain stylistic cues present in the wider text to assure us that what we read is intended as humorous and laughter is an appropriate response to what we see. The reason why many instances of humour in narratives are so bound to their context is that, in order to fully appreciate them, we need to encounter them as part of a textual world which, based on the cues present in the text, we perceive as generally humorous. In my previous work, I suggested that the narrative worlds of many comic novels and films are constructed as *humorous worlds* (Marszalek 2013, 2016a, b). Designed with the use of a range of cues which signal the humorous quality of the world, humorous worlds elicit an overall impression of humour in the reader – an impression which can enhance the humorous potential of the individual elements that appear in the world. The amusing quality of such elements is context-dependent, meaning that it is the wider context which helps to 'unlock' the humour in them for the receiver.

In the process of reading, we encounter numerous stylistic 'cues': those elements of the linguistic layer of the text which signal (and perhaps elicit) emotional responses. In comic narratives, these cues can shape our emotional responses to the three experiential components of the humorous worlds which the texts encourage us to inhabit:

1. the moods evoked by being in the world,
2. our feelings for text-based characters, and
3. our reactions to narrative plot events.

While many of these cues will be designed to evoke amusement and therefore create our impression of the world as a humorous one, a large proportion of them will signal responses which are associated not with humour, but rather with our emotional engagement with the narrative world more generally.

1.2. Distance and immersion: Stabilizing and destabilizing comedy

Our experience of comic novels and short stories is guided by two disparate forces: *distance* and *immersion*. While distancing the reader from the characters and events described is associated with humour creation, reducing that distance and encouraging us to immerse ourselves in the textual world can disrupt the experience of humour. In order to cue humorous distance and non-humorous immersion, comic narratives rely on two types of stylistic feature which either stabilize or destabilize our experience of comedy:

Stabilizing cues

Stylistic features of comic narratives which signal amusement and stabilize our experience of comedy. They distance us from the narrative world to encourage a detached, playful, sometimes mocking attitude towards the world.

Destabilizing cues

Stylistic features of comic narratives which signal non-humorous emotions that destabilize our experience of comedy. They lead us to immerse ourselves in the narrative world and form feelings and attachments for its entities.

Stabilizing cues can be understood as those elements of the linguistic layer of the text which can be expected to evoke amusement, and which, through frequent use, contribute to our perception of the narrative world as one which is generally humorous. The close link between humour and amusement is a notion that underlies much of the psychological research on the emotional aspects of humour, where the term *amusement* (and the synonymous mirth, hilarity, cheerfulness or merriment) is used to describe the positive emotion closely related to joy, elicited by a perception that a situation is funny (Martin 2007: 8). Its experiential qualities are associated with feelings of pleasure – amusement is, as Martin suggests, that 'unique feeling of well-being' familiar to all of us (2007: 8). Like other emotions, amusement can be said to be elicited by our cognitive appraisal of an encountered stimulus (e.g. Arnold 1961; Frijda 1986 and 2007). In order to evoke amusement, therefore, verbal stimuli such as humorous texts need to contain linguistic elements which are evaluated as humorous – in the case of written comic narratives, those elements will be the particular stylistic cues appraised by readers as amusing. Based on philosophical, linguistic and psychological work on humour, the amusing effect of those cues will be associated with our responses to *incongruity*, and

Table 1 Stabilizing and destabilizing cues in comic narratives

Cue	Function in humorous world		Emotional response in reader	
	Creation	Experience	Individual	Combined
Stabilizing	Creates comedy	Distance from narrative world	Amusement	Complex humorous response
Destabilizing	Disrupts comedy	Immersion in narrative world	Non-humorous emotion	

specifically, incongruity which is appraised in a non-serious, playful cognitive state of detachment from ordinary concerns. The chapters that follow outline how text-based incongruity, manipulations of narrative distance and other stylistic features can act as stabilizing cues which shape our impression of the moods, characters and events in narrative worlds as amusing, thus establishing our experience of those worlds as humorous.

While, perhaps predictably, amusement-inducing cues stabilize our experience of comedy, comic narratives additionally contain elements which destabilize the comic experience by evoking emotions not typically associated with humour. Those non-humorous emotions stem from our engagement with the characters and situations which make up the narrative world of the text – engagement which is facilitated by our immersion in that world. From an upsetting mood triggered by emotionally charged, evocative language of a passage, to the experience of embarrassment on behalf of a character, to a tense, anxious feeling as a response to a suspenseful story event, non-humorous emotional states are responses which stem from our involvement in the narrative. Such unpleasant emotions have the potential to destabilize the otherwise positive experiential quality of humorous worlds. Importantly, however, in the context of reading comic narratives, emotions otherwise seen as negative will often add to the entertaining quality of the humorous world of the text. The highly desired state of 'being in' a narrative world (whether humorous or not) does not, after all, exclude experiences that are inherently unpleasant. In fact, we are often drawn to story worlds which allow us to explore the boundaries of our resilience to fear, sadness or anger (Green, Brock and Kaufman 2004: 315), and enjoy such responses in a cathartic context (Miall 2007: 81).

Narrative comedy is a balancing act between distancing the readers from the textual world so as to enable them to perceive it as laughable, and immersing them in the world of the text in order to maintain an interest in the story. While the distancing stabilizing cues and the immersive destabilizing cues can occur independently and lead to either amusement or a non-humorous emotion in the process of reading a comic narrative, the experience of a humorous world is based in part on what will be referred to as a *complex humorous response*, which is a combination of the two. A complex humorous response – a blend of amusement and a non-humorous emotion – can be evoked when a destabilizing cue is introduced to a part of a narrative context otherwise stabilized as humorous. It is when the two types of cue are presented simultaneously that a complex humorous response can occur. A complex humorous response, simply put, is the reason why some narratives (or their passages) can be described by readers as simultaneously funny *and* heartbreaking – as illustrated by the reader of *A Spot of Bother* in her review of the novel quoted above.

1.3. This book

This work offers a predominantly stylistic, world-based approach to the language of comic novels and short stories, complemented by discussions of real readers' online comments about their experience of reading those texts. While I address the issue of the experience – as shaped by stylistic cues – of whole, full-length narratives in the course of reading, my argument is based on analyses of short narrative extracts chosen from the books. Those passages were selected as they exemplify the types of cue that, as I have found in my analysis of a number of texts, commonly reoccur in the comic novels and short stories which were analysed:

Adams, D. ([1979] 2002), *The Hitchhiker's Guide to the Galaxy*, London: Picador.
Fielding, H. ([1996] 1998), *Bridget Jones's Diary*, London: Picador.
Haddon, M. (2007), *A Spot of Bother*, London: Vintage.
Heller, J. ([1961] 1994), *Catch-22*, London: Vintage.
Hornby, N. (1995), *High Fidelity*, London: Penguin.
Jerome, J. K. ([1889] 1993), *Three Men in a Boat (To Say Nothing of the Dog!)*, Ware: Wordsworth Editions Limited.

Lewycka, M. ([2005] 2006), *A Short History of Tractors in Ukrainian*, London: Penguin.
Milligan, S. (1971), *Adolf Hitler: My Part in His Downfall*, London: Michael Joseph Ltd.
Sedaris, D. ([2000] 2002), *Me Talk Pretty One Day*, London: Abacus.
Townsend, S. ([1982] 2002), *The Secret Diary of Adrian Mole, Aged 13¾*, London: Puffin.
Wodehouse, P. G. ([1934] 2008), *Right Ho, Jeeves*, London: Arrow Books.

While the analysis of the narrative examples is mostly language-based, it opens the discussion to more psychologically motivated considerations of the potential experiential qualities of the stylistic organization of the text. In this book, theories and concepts from various branches of psychology (most notably, psychology of humour and psychological approaches to literature, film and television) are applied to the stylistic analysis of humorous extracts to explore the potential emotional effects of the language of comic narratives. Psychological research on, among others, negative affect, embarrassment and suspense is also discussed in relation to the non-humorous experiential qualities of humorous worlds, thereby allowing me to pose hypotheses which inform the core of this study.

In order to further support those hypotheses, I occasionally refer to real readers' comments about their emotional experience of the narratives analysed here. The comments are extracts from reviews of those narratives submitted for the online reading community Goodreads between 2007 (the year of its launch) and 2015 – these have been anonymized for ethical reasons, but they are publicly accessible under the 'Community Reviews' headings on the main Goodreads page of each book. My choice of Goodreads posts as reader response data is informed by the approach taken by Gavins (2013) in her account of the experience of reading the literary absurd. Her study, although based primarily on a stylistic analysis and her own subjective responses to absurdist texts, includes references to readers' comments about those texts gathered from a number of websites. A consideration of such naturally occurring, pre-existing reviews in which readers voluntarily share their experience of full-length literary works with each other online, as Gavins argues, falls within what Swann and Allington (2009: 248) term naturalistic studies of reader response (Gavins 2013: 7, see also Peplow and Carter 2014; Peplow et al. 2015). In contrast to experimental studies, which tend to focus on pre-specified interpretative activities, and in which 'the need for experimental control leads to rather artificial reading behaviour being investigated, with readers interacting with atypical texts', naturalistic studies concern habitual processes of reading whole texts in their typical form (Swann and Allington 2009: 248). Although my study is based predominantly on a linguistic analysis of written narratives supported by insights from psychology, it does pose hypotheses about habitual reading of full-length texts. A naturalistic investigation of a number of online reader responses therefore complements my cognitive stylistic analysis and discussions of psychological theories, providing additional evidence about the experience of reading comic narratives.

This book combines linguistic tools and theories with research in psychology, literary/film/television studies and various perspectives on humour in order to offer an interdisciplinary – although rooted in linguistics – approach to the study of the experience of the narrative worlds of comic novels and short stories. The following chapters explore particular aspects of that experience: the moods evoked in us as we read, the attachments and feelings which we are encouraged to build for the characters, and the reactions which the presentation of plot events can trigger in us. Each of these will be discussed independently (in Chapters 3, 4 and 5, respectively), following Chapter 2, which provides a background to some of the theoretical concepts which underlie this study.

In Chapter 2, 'Narrative worlds, literary emotion and humorous discourse', I outline both the world-based approaches to written discourse comprehension relevant to cognitive stylistics and the psychological work which concerns readers' immersion in the worlds of literature. I review some of the psychological and literary linguistic approaches to readers' emotional engagement with literary and media texts, and discuss both the relevant research within the study of humour as a whole, and those concepts within the linguistics of humour that will be drawn on in this book.

In Chapter 3, 'Experiencing modes and moods', I consider the ways in which writers of comic narratives prepare the reader for the experience of humour by cueing particular cognitive and affective predispositions. I suggest that engaging with comic texts most likely leads to amusement when the reader has a cognitive awareness that the text is intended to be amusing and an affective sense that the text is amusing. These states of humorous expectation, referred to as the *humorous mode* and the *humorous mood*, respectively, will be said to stabilize the experience of comedy by facilitating amusement in the reader. In the chapter, I outline a number of stylistic devices which help to cue the humorous predisposition, as well as techniques which disrupt the mode/mood, thus destabilizing our experience of comedy and resulting in complex humorous responses. Among these complex responses, I focus primarily on *dark humour* and show the stylistic techniques used to create it.

Chapter 4, 'Engaging with characters', focuses on the role of characterization in narrative humour creation. I discuss the techniques which allow representations of people in humorous narrative worlds to have a comic effect, thus stabilizing the reader's experience of comedy. I outline a number of character stock types present in comic narratives and suggest a complex type who combines a number of amusing features – the *misfit*. In the second part of the chapter, I contrast the laughable misfit with another type, the sympathetic *everyman/everywoman*, to show how imbuing protagonists with an amalgamation of misfit/every(wo)man qualities can manipulate the reader's response to the situations they find themselves in, potentially destabilizing our experience of humour. I discuss the stylistic devices associated with the creation of *cringe comedy*, where embarrassment on behalf of characters is cued alongside amusement targeted at their ineptitude.

In Chapter 5, 'Reacting to story structures', I consider the ways in which the presentation of story events affects our experience of humorous narrative worlds. I discuss a typical trajectory of a comic plot and concentrate on the notion of a *humorous complication*: a surprising story event which is unfortunate to the character but – thanks to our ability to distance ourselves from its emotional impact and reach a *humorous resolution* – humorous to the reader. While *comic surprise* which accompanies humorous complications is said to stabilize our amusement and experience of comedy, *comic suspense* is seen as a more uncomfortable, destabilizing reaction. In the second part of the chapter, therefore, I suggest some of the techniques that allow writers to create this suspense by delaying the presentation of a negative outcome which the reader has already been led to anticipate.

Finally, Chapter 6, 'Conclusion', provides a summary of the main ideas introduced in this book, specifically the notion of stylistic cues stabilizing and destabilizing the reader's experience of the narrative worlds of comic texts, and the ability of those cues to either immerse the reader in the world or distance him or her from it. Following an overview of how those themes were explored in the individual chapters, I provide a detailed list of the particular stylistic cues which are used in comic narratives, as well as their potential emotional effects.

2

Narrative worlds, literary emotion and humorous discourse

This book is a linguistic account of the stylistic features of comic novels and short stories. While the focus is on the language of comedy, the linguistic analysis is undertaken here with a view to identifying those elements of written comic texts which can shape our experience of reading. The overall approach is, therefore, interdisciplinary: it draws not only on linguistic work on humour, but also on research in psychology, philosophy, literary/film/television studies, as well as cognitive perspectives on literary comprehension and emotion. This chapter provides a background to the main theoretical directions of this work, focusing on relevant approaches to the cognitive and affective aspects of reading (2.1.) and select perspectives on humour and the language of comedy (2.2.).

2.1. Cognitive and affective aspects of reading

Behind the words of any novel or short story, there is a *narrative world* that comes into existence in the course of reading the text. That world is a mental representation of the space outlined by the narrative, constructed partly from the linguistic elements present in the text, and partly from the readers' own cognitive and affective mechanisms.

2.1.1. World-based approaches to discourse comprehension

The decision to associate written narratives with the worlds they allow us to build in our minds is based on those approaches to discourse which emphasize the role of the narrative context in text comprehension. That context, here referred to as a narrative world, is a concept informed by existing literary and linguistic research in narrative and discourse processing.

Some of the early world-based approaches to literature arose as a response to the problem of fictionality in philosophy, which concerned the complicated ontological and logical status of fictional characters, events and settings. Although the non-actual entities present in literary fictions can be considered to exist in the works of fiction to which they belong, their existence is not as straightforward in the real world where the fiction is being read. A solution to this ontological uncertainty was proposed by applying the philosophical concept of *possible worlds* to the legitimation of fictional beings and situations (e.g. Ryan 1980; Pavel 1986; Doležel 1989, see also Semino 1997). The possible-world framework was based on the idea that the world we perceive as real is simply one of the limitless number of alternative' universes. The fictional worlds of literature, therefore, have been defined as sets of possible states of affairs that are unlimited, maximally varied, and accessible from the actual world in which the literature is being read (Doležel 1989: 230–2). Aside from being accessible to readers from the real world, as Ryan suggests, fictional worlds will be construed by us 'as being the closest possible to the reality we know' (Ryan 1980: 406). What she terms *the principle of minimal departure* signifies readers' tendency to project their knowledge of the actual world onto the world of fiction, making adjustments only when absolutely necessary (Ryan 1980: 406).

A model of discourse comprehension which develops this distinction between readers' general knowledge of the real world and their text-based knowledge of the fictional world of a narrative is Emmott's (1994, 1997) *contextual frame theory* (although she additionally distinguishes between readers' knowledge of typical text structures and knowledge of the style of a particular text, 1997: 21). A *contextual frame*, meaning 'a mental store of information about the current context, built up from the text itself and from inferences made from the text' (1997: 121), is a building-block of what Emmott refers to as *text-specific knowledge* – the information about textual entities accumulated in the course of reading (1997: 35). Contextual frames, which readers keep track of through an active form of memory called *contextual monitoring* (1997: 106), provide information about the precise configurations of characters, locations and times at various points in a narrative. Narrative comprehension, therefore, relies on readers' ability to monitor the narrative context in order to construct a mental representation of the textual world as a whole.

The idea of a mental model of a text-driven context, together with the focus on the non-actual world outlined by discourse, lies at the heart of *text world theory* (Werth 1999, developed by Gavins 2007). Here, a distinction is made between the actual world in which the reading takes place, the *discourse world*, and the world constructed in the course of reading, the *text world* (Werth 1999: 17). Both the immediate situation of the discourse world and the textual situation of the text world, as Werth suggests, contain the same basic types of elements, such as characters, objects, place and time (1999: 81–2). The text world – the 'conceptual space into which the discourse refers' (Werth 1999: 48) – is created as a negotiation between discourse participants (e.g. the writer and the reader), based partly on the linguistic elements present in the text, and partly on the participants' own knowledge which allows them to build a mental space of the textual situation represented in the discourse.

2.1.2. Emotion and the experience of literary narrative

Aside from creating mental representations of textual worlds in the course of reading, readers are also said to have an opportunity to 'visit fictional lands, inhabit them for a while' (Pavel 1986: 85). The idea of readers visiting or inhabiting narrative spaces was developed by Gerrig (1993), who emphasized the distinction between a narrative (a text with some formal features) and the experience of a narrative world (a result of a set of mental operations). Gerrig suggests that the experience of a narrative world relies on the reader 'being in' the space to which the narrative refers. One of the metaphors used to characterize this experience is that of *transportation*, understood as a temporary departure from the real world: 'readers', according to Gerrig, 'are often described as *being transported* by a narrative' (Gerrig 1993: 2). Aside from transportation, psychological and cognitive approaches to reading offer a range of metaphors to describe readers' experience of 'entering' the narrative worlds of literature: from *immersion* or *absorption* in a story (Nell 1988; Green 2010; Green and Brock 2000), to *recentering*, where the reader is pushed into a fictional world as a result of immersion in a work of fiction (Ryan 1991), and *decentering*, meaning shifting away from our own lives as a result of our interest in the lives of fictional characters (Miall 2007).

As far as more specific emotional responses to narratives are concerned, the main theoretical direction adopted in this book has been laid out in Sanford and Emmott's (2012) *Rhetorical Processing Framework*, where the primary subject of investigation is the nature of the mental processing operations that account for our ability to comprehend narrative texts. Experiencing narratives, according to Sanford and Emmott, relies on narrative comprehension being complemented by processes from the two broad classes of *embodiment* and *emotion*, which enrich our understanding of texts with aspects of what the authors call *experientiality*. Embodiment here refers to the idea that while reading, we draw on our bodily, sensory experience, which is said to sometimes enable us to imagine that we are performing the actions described in the text (see Kuzmičová 2012 for a discussion of this or Gibbs 2005 for a general approach to embodiment theory). Emotion, the other aspect of experientiality, is said to interact with the cognitive processes involved in reading so as to 'colour and modify' them in what Sanford and Emmott refer to as *hot cognition*. The three components of hot cognition discussed by them are (1) general emotional judgements and feelings evoked by texts, (2) empathy for characters and (3) the emotions of suspense, surprise and curiosity elicited by story structures (2012: 191–232).

This idea of interconnectedness of cognition and emotion in reading developed in Sanford and Emmott's work also forms the core of Miall's (e.g. 1995, 2007) research on the role of feeling in experiencing literature (where 'literature' includes narratives, but refers to 'high culture' texts which exhibit the elite quality of *literariness*). Among other things, Miall is interested in literature's ability to allow us to consider various ways of both thinking about the world and being in the world – for example, by offering us a safe way of experimenting with experiences and feelings that might have dangerous or dire consequences in real life (2007: 17). Experiencing emotions related to unpleasant events, in fact, features prominently in Miall's approach to literary response. He classifies finding pleasure in negative feelings as one of the key features of feeling in literary reading (2007: 81) and links it to Aristotle's notion of *catharsis* (releasing difficult emotions through art), associated with the genre of tragedy (1995: 292). While Miall maintains that people do generally read literature as they anticipate the experience to be pleasurable (due to, for example, vivid imagery or plot twists), the process of reading places unpleasant, negative emotions in a critical context, allowing us a deeper understanding of them.

2.2. Humour studies and the language of comedy

Although this work explores, quite broadly, the role of emotion in our experience of narrative worlds, it is primarily an interdisciplinary study of comic narratives. As such, it draws from a range of philosophical, psychological and linguistic approaches to both humour generally, and comic novels and short stories specifically.

2.2.1. Schools of thought

Research in humour studies is traditionally separated into three main groups of theories: superiority, release and incongruity theories.

Although the linguistics of humour is generally associated with the sub-class of incongruity, each of the three groups provide insights into the emotional aspects of humorous text comprehension.

(i) Superiority theories

The superiority theories within humour studies are concerned with humour as a means of disparaging other individuals, and the feeling of superiority associated with mocking others' shortcomings and misfortunes. The origins of this disparagement-based approach to humour date back to the philosophical works of Plato, Aristotle and Socrates (in Billig 2005: 40; Ermida 2008: 21). The role of the feeling of superiority in humour appreciation has been linked to Hobbes, whose term *sudden glory* ([1651] 1996: 43) relates to the unexpected boost of self-congratulation which is said to lie at the heart of our pleasure in humour. While Hobbes stresses the importance of the feeling of superiority in those who laugh, the work of Bergson (1913: 22–3) contains references to the amusing value of the deformity and ugliness in those who are laughed at. These early views of humour as aggressive and morally suspicious can be seen to have lost some of their relevance in the present-day context. That is why, rather than treating all humour as an expression of hostility, researchers now tend to speak of different types of humour, where the superiority-based kind is referred to as *disparagement humour*: a genre which includes slapstick, racist, sexist or practical jokes (e.g. Ferguson and Ford 2008, see also Martin 2007: 45).

(ii) Release theories

The release theories of humour (also referred to as arousal or relief theories) see humour as deriving from a sense of psychological relief which follows a release of some form of tension. The origins of this approach can be linked to Spencer's (1860) view of laughter as a means of releasing built-up excess nervous energy. A version of this view of the human nervous system as a mechanism for regulating nervous energy has been further developed by Freud, who proposed the concept of *psychical expenditure* required for creating and maintaining psychical inhibitions ([1905] 1960: 145). Humour, according to Freud, relies on some form of energy (often the energy needed to suppress forbidden emotions such as aggression or sexual desire) to be saved and subsequently released together with laughter. This release satisfies the longing for freedom from the constraints imposed on the individual by the society, and therefore is seen as a source of pleasure. Since both Freud's psychoanalytic theory and Spencer's energy-release approach have been largely discredited by modern psychology (Martin 2007: 41, 58), it may be unsurprising that the related contemporary release-based approach to humour, Berlyne's (e.g. 1972) notion of *arousal jag*, has not been supported by physiological research data (Martin 2007: 60).

(iii) Incongruity theories
Incongruity theories – most applicable, as will be shown further, to the linguistics of humour – stress the role of incongruity in the humorous stimulus and the experience of that incongruity for the receiver. This school of thought is often associated with the work of Schopenhauer, who described laughter as a response to encountering an unexpected combination of some contrasting features under a single point of view ([1819] 1969: 59). While the incongruous nature of humorous objects is an axiom shared by incongruity-based theories, the mechanisms behind the processing of this incongruity have been debated (e.g. Forabosco 2008). It has been questioned whether amusement can be triggered by the mere perception of incongruity (like in the case of *nonsense humour*, e.g. Morreall 1987b; Mulkay 1988, see also Gavins 2013: 50 for a discussion of this in *absurd humour*), or whether humour lies in hearers' *resolution* of the incongruity with which they are presented (e.g. Suls 1972).

2.2.2. Linguistic approaches to humour

Linguistic perspectives on humour often draw on the idea of incongruity in the humorous text. A highly influential and productive approach to the humorous incongruity found in verbal jokes is Raskin's (1985)

Semantic Script Theory of Humor (*SSTH*). A key term in the theory is a *semantic script*, which is to be understood as a chunk of semantic information evoked by some part of the text. The basic premise of SSTH is that:

> A text can be characterized as a single-joke-carrying text if both of the conditions are satisfied:
>
> (i) The text is compatible, fully or in part, with two different scripts;
> (ii) The two scripts with which the text is compatible are opposite in a special sense.
>
> (Raskin 1985: 99)

As far as the 'special sense' is concerned, jokes are said to evoke such binary categories as good versus bad, true versus false or, on the most general level, real versus unreal (1985: 113). A joke, then, is a text that describes a certain 'real' situation and evokes another 'unreal' situation which does not in fact occur and which is not compatible with the former (1985: 108).

Raskin's SSTH, which originated as a semantic theory of jokes, subsequently developed into a more comprehensive model intended to be applicable to all verbal humour, from short jokes to humour found in longer texts. This development, Attardo and Raskin's (1991) *General Theory of Verbal Humor* (*GTVH*), identifies six 'parameters of joke difference' (despite its apparent relevance to all verbal humour, the authors base their theory on jokes) known as *knowledge resources* (*KRs*), which are said to inform a joke (Attardo and Raskin 1991: 297–309). Each KR represents a number of choices which have to be made for a joke to be conceived. A typical joke, as the authors suggest, will include a certain choice of script opposition (SO), a logical mechanism (LM), a situation (SI), a target (TA), a narrative strategy (NS) and language (LA). The same joke can take on different forms depending on the choices made within each KR, and the application of the theory relies mainly on identifying each KR for the joke which is analysed.

2.2.2.1. Linguistic approaches to narrative humour

(i) Attardo

Attardo's application of GTVH to more complex texts, including narratives (Attardo 1998, 2001), provides a way of analysing a range of humorous features of written texts of any length by identifying all of their humorous elements. Those elements, *jab lines*, can then be analysed by describing them according to the KR criteria (as is done with jokes) in a way which can help draw parallels and identify relationships between all the lines in a text. Attardo's notions of *strands* (lines which are somehow related, for example, share one of the same KRs), *bridges* (occurrences of two related lines far from each other) and *combs* (occurrences of several lines close to each other) form a terminology for describing the structure of any text which features at least a few instances of humour (2002: 241, 236).

(ii) Ermida

Ermida's (2008) approach to the construction of humour in short stories can be seen to have been influenced by the work of Raskin and Attardo. Her comprehensive study of the language of comic narratives includes an outline of a range of linguistic resources of humour (e.g. sound, graphology, morpho-syntax, semantics), as well as the applications of a narrative structure and pragmatic analysis to the study of narrative humour. In her model of humorous narratives, she proposes a number of principles which need to be obeyed if a text is to be classified as humorous: *Principle of Opposition* (each script processed in the text activates an opposite script), *Principle of Hierarchy* (those scripts are divided into higher supra-scripts and lower infra-scripts), *Principle of Recurrence* (the supra-scripts are recurrently instantiated, which leads readers to form predictions and expectations), *Principle of Informativeness* (the ending of the story involves an unexpected breaking of those expectations) and *Principle of Cooperation* (this contradiction of built-up expectations carries a cooperative intention of comicality on the writer's part) (2008: 172–3).

(iii) Triezenberg

The SSTH- and GTVH-inspired models of narrative humour provide insights into the illocutionary force and the structural aspects of extended comic narratives. In her theory of *humour enhancers* in comic literature, Triezenberg (2004, 2008) challenges those semantic approaches to argue that literary humour should not be reduced to a simple analysis of KRs in particular lines. She suggests that while humorous jab lines are present in comic literature, their full comic potential is best realized when it is enhanced by specific techniques present in the texts – humour enhancers:

> A humor enhancer is a narrative technique that is not necessarily funny in and of itself, but that helps an audience to understand that the text is supposed to be funny, that warms them up to the author and to the text so that they will be more receptive to humor, and that magnifies their experience of humor in the text.
>
> (Triezenberg 2008: 538)

The list of enhancers which add to the reader's experience of humour in the narrative includes unusual *diction*, easily accessible *shared stereotypes*, *cultural factors* related to the reader's general knowledge, *repetition and variation* of the same joke and, finally, *familiarity*, which puts the reader at ease by reducing the tension around processing new information.

(iv) Larkin Galiñanes

Larkin Galiñanes (2000) applies relevance theory to the study of humorous narratives to argue that comic novels, unlike 'high' literature, rely on a repetition of certain salient connotations that can be used in the construction of predictable, comic *character-stereotypes* and generating surprising *internal incongruity*, the resolution of which is a source of satisfaction for the reader. In her analysis of Kingsley Amis' *Lucky Jim* (2002), she additionally draws on the superiority theories within humour studies to suggest the role of *attitudinal positioning* in guiding the reader's identification (either positive or negative) with chosen characters. Her more recent work (2010) shows how insights from each of the three schools within humour studies can benefit the study of literary humour. She draws on each of the groups to suggest how *superiority* is fuelled by readers' negative identification with particular characters, how sequences of events build up tension which is then *released* through humour, and how some character-related *incongruity* can be resolved with reference to the knowledge we already have about the character.

(v) Nash

In his comprehensive study of the language of humour, Nash (1985) proposes the term *humorous expansion* for the humour present in long comic texts, as distinguished from *witty compression* found in short jokes and puns. Humorous expansion has three modes, or qualities: *generic, linguistic* and *interactional,* where generic refers to the literary and cultural context, linguistic to patterns of syntax, semantics and sound, and interactional to the relationship between the executant and the respondent (1985: 21). The design of extended comic narratives, according to Nash, additionally relies on three features which are brought to the reader's attention: the *locative formula*, the *formulate* and the *root joke* (1985: 70). The locative formula is a formulaic joke which can be found, for example, in character speech, especially as an attribute of a funny character. A formulate is, similarly, a humorous comment, but a comment which is expressed by the author or 'external' narrator. A root joke, finally, is one which informs the whole infrastructure of the narrative – a joke of which the reader is regularly reminded. As far as the overall relationship between language and humour in comedy is concerned, Nash makes a distinction between 'the language of comedy' and 'humorous language', where the latter refers to the stylistic qualities of particular sentences, phrases or words, and the former is a broader concept that concerns 'a discursive relationship between all the parts of a text and its infrastructure' (1985: 126). The two terms are not, of course, mutually exclusive, as any utterance can be described as both 'humorous' and 'comedic' (Nash 1985: 126).

2.3. Summary

Unlike the linguistic models mentioned above, my approach to comic narratives is not limited to the study of humour – and especially, not limited to seeking those structural features of humorous texts which render the texts humorous. While humour is my concern, I view humorous amusement as simply one of the emotional reactions cued by the stylistic techniques that shape our experience of humorous novels and short stories. I am therefore interested in how those linguistic elements which contribute to our perception of the narratives as humorous interact with those components which can be expected to cue very different, often negative, emotional responses. This book, consequently, moves beyond the study of the creation and comprehension of humorous language to an investigation of the affective side of comic narrative processing – one that is shaped by the stylistic world-building techniques used to create the narrative worlds of humorous novels and short stories.

3
Experiencing modes and moods

There are a number of factors which can shape our emotional experience of reading. One of these is the sense of expectation evoked in us by a particular novel or short story; in many ways, our reactions to a text will be affected by what we anticipate to feel in response to it. Whether or not a comic narrative triggers our amusement, therefore, will be partly dependent on the writer's ability to guide our humorous interpretation of the text by creating an anticipation of humour. This chapter shows how the stylistic cues which help to establish this sense of humorous expectation in comic narratives can be said to have the stabilizing effect of providing a larger humorous context in which the emotion of amusement is established as a preferred, dominant response. Some cues, however, will destabilize the comic context by evoking a more serious mood, thus triggering, potentially, complex humorous responses. It is the balance between the stabilizing and the destabilizing cues present in the text which determines a reader's overall experience of a humorous narrative world.

3.1. Theoretical background

The idea of the reader's expectation central to this chapter draws on the literary and linguistic research on concepts such as *atmosphere*, *tone* and *ambience* as qualities of literary and media texts, as well as notions like *play*, *paratelic* or *humorous mode*, *frame* or *key* as aspects of humorous communication discussed in both pragmatics and psychology of humour. These kinds of considerations, however, need to be complemented by a general discussion of *mood* as it is broadly defined in psychology. That is because my focus is on the emotional experience of reading, and the manipulations of the reader's mood are essential to this experience.

3.1.1. The psychology of mood

Psychological research views mood as an evaluative mental state which can predispose one to act according to its affective content (Parkinson et al. 1996: 9–10). The evaluative component of mood means that, in contrast to what could be described as a purely cognitive frame of mind, mood is seen as an *affective state* which can be felt as good or bad (Parkinson 1995: 4). Affective states can be distinguished from each other on the basis of a number of dimensions, but the *pleasantness-unpleasantness* polarity seems to feature in a number of models of affective structure (e.g. Russell 1980; Watson and Tellegen 1985). Affect, whether positive or negative, is not restricted to moods. In psychological literature, mood is most frequently defined through comparison with emotion – both of which are classified as affective states.

The one marked feature of moods which is most relevant to literary linguistics is that of moods being *tonic* states. While emotions appear and vanish rapidly, moods are said to set a background tone of experience which remains relatively stable (Parkinson 1995: 9). This idea of mood being a stable affective background influencing an individual's interpretation of events, when applied to literature, can be seen to be related to Miall's (1995) notion of *affective tone*, which, once established, will have a long-term effect on subsequent reading. Affect in literary reading, according to Miall, is 'anticipatory', meaning that it pre-structures our understanding of the text early in the reading process (1989: 56). The anticipatory quality of affect shapes our interpretation of literary texts. Once a certain tone has been set up, the reader will be predisposed to comprehending the text in concordance with that particular feeling.

3.1.2. Mood in literary and film studies

In literary criticism, the term 'mood' is rarely used on its own merit, but rather as an auxiliary to describe two other concepts – *atmosphere* and *tone* of literary texts. Even a basic review of a number of dictionaries of literary terms reveals that not only are both atmosphere and tone defined as moods evoked by literature, but that the three concepts can in fact be used interchangeably (e.g. Baldick 2008: 336; Abrams and Harpman 2012: 18–9). Atmosphere and tone are described as qualities of texts rather than those of readers, yet they seem to generally refer to the way a literary work makes us feel: the mood it evokes in us.

Stylistics and narratology focus on the notion of tone to suggest, for example, that a certain overall tone (e.g. ironic, intimate) can be adopted by the narrator or the implied author as part of the *modality* (or *point of view*, Genette 1980) of the work (Wales 2011: 425). A comprehensive stylistic account of tone has been developed by Leech and Short (2007: 225–9), who, like Wales, link it to *discoursal point of view*, which they see as the relationship between the implied author (or other addresser) and the fiction, expressed through the structure of the discourse. Part of this relationship is the *authorial tone*, that is, the position taken by the (implied) author towards the readers, and towards the message (2007: 225). An important consideration here is that of symmetry between the attitude expressed by the author and that evoked in the reader (which may be close, but not complete), and the related notion of *distance*. Leech and Short distinguish between two types of distance: that between the writer and the reader, related to the perceived feeling of familiarity between them, and that between the writer and the subject matter, based on the writer's sympathy towards elements of the world portrayed by him or her (Leech and Short 2007: 225–6). Tone is an expression of this distance, which, when inferred by the reader, can potentially create a particular mood.

A more encompassing approach to tone has been proposed by Stockwell (2014), who acknowledges the association between tone and the concept of authorial/narratorial voice, but who nevertheless recognizes the close relationship between tone and atmosphere. The terms 'tone' and 'atmosphere', Stockwell notes, basing his view on an analysis of entries from the British National Corpus, both tend to be used in an imprecise, impressionistic sense, generally referring to a certain emotional quality of a passage of a literary text. For the purpose of cognitive stylistic analysis, he accordingly proposes *ambience* as a superordinate term for both words (2014: 365). Ambience is distinguished from *resonance* (Stockwell 2009) in that while resonance is the striking, powerful feeling which persists after the reading, ambience is the effect of an accumulation of associations created across the discourse itself.

The stylistic approaches to mood, atmosphere and tone mentioned above all relate to literary works and their readers, but these notions can also be applied to other, multimodal, texts. Smith's (2003) *mood-cue approach to filmic emotion* relies on the idea that film narratives cue moods (lower-level emotional states) in their viewers in order to predispose them to experiencing brief moments of strong emotion in the course of watching. Films need to provide a variety and abundance of *mood cues* to sustain the particular emotional background which will guide their viewers' mental processing in the direction desired by the production crew. That direction will involve brief moments of emotion elicited by *emotion markers*, which prompt feelings congruent with the overall mood that is being sustained. Smith points out that particular genres have their own patterns of emotional address encoded as *genre microscripts* that will guide our expectations as to how a certain film is likely to progress narratively, but that there exist *genre blends* which rely on mixes of moods and cues (for example *Ghostbusters* is a blend of comedy and horror, Smith 2003: 49–51). The idea of these types of blend will be relevant in the final section of this chapter, where I discuss the ability of writers to achieve special effects by cueing a range of different, sometimes incongruent, moods within a comic narrative.

3.1.3. Humour studies approaches to mode

While moods can be linked to genres, as Smith suggests, it will be shown further that the blends of moods found in comic texts mean that the 'genre of comedy' is perhaps a slightly problematic term. Accordingly, King (2002) proposes that (film) comedy is best understood as a *mode* of representation, rather than a genre. This mode is established through comedy-specific modality markers which, although prone to variations and shifts, act so as to create a sense of distance from reality and/or seriousness (King 2002: 9). There will be times, argues King, when comedy is allowed to dominate the overall tone of the film, but there also exist comedies which encourage the mixing and shifts of tone, or indeed serious films where comic elements are used to create disruption and an imbalance of moods. Comedy as a mode of a text is also discussed by Mulkay (1988), who distinguishes between the *serious mode* and the *humorous mode* of discourse. 'The requirements of acceptable discourse,' argues Mulkay, 'vary from one mode to another' (1988: 21): while the humorous mode is much less restrictive with regards to standards of consistency, coherence and feasibility than the serious mode, it does require certain levels of ambiguity, contradiction and interpretative duality.

Another type of mode discussed by humour theorists is that not of the text, but of the receiver of humorous discourse. Morreall (2009) argues that humour is a sudden change of mental state (a *cognitive shift*) experienced in a *play mode*, that is, when we are disengaged from ordinary, practical concerns. Incongruity does not invariably lead to humour – it is most likely to trigger amusement when, as Morreall (1987b) suggests, we are not practically engaged in it and therefore do not feel a loss of control. The idea of being in a play mode when engaging in humorous activities is closely related to the reversal theory approach to humour (Apter 1982, 1991), according to which amusement is associated with a playful, *paratelic* state of mind of the participant. Unlike the goal-oriented *telic* state, paratelic state is linked to various forms of play, where the primary motivation behind performing activities is not the completion of a task, but the act of engaging in the activity itself. As Martin points out in his comprehensive review of psychological literature on humour, 'the view of humor as play reminds us that humor is a nonserious, playful activity that differs from more serious modes of thinking' (2007: 81).

While psychology of humour focuses on mode as the frame of mind of the hearer, other disciplines, including linguistic pragmatics, provide approaches which stress the position of the speaker in eliciting that state in the recipient of humorous communication. Dynel (2011) outlines a number of ways in which participants in conversations provide cues as to whether their utterances are to be interpreted in a *humorous* or *play frame*. This idea of a play frame is linked to Bateson's (e.g. [1972] 2006) notion of meta-communication surrounding play activities, where play is required to be accompanied by signals that carry the meta-message 'this is play' for it to be successfully carried out by participants. Using humour in conversation, according to Dynel, involves this kind of *humorous framing* or *keying*. She points out, however, that the humorous and non-humorous frames are prone to merging – depending on their balance, utterances can range from purely humorous to non-humorous ones imbued with humour (Dynel 2011: 228).

In the context of written comic narratives, this type of framing will be related to the ways in which authors communicate the *intention of comicality* (Ermida 2008) to their readers. As I will argue throughout, many elements which appear in humorous narrative worlds are not immediately amusing, but become humorous to the reader who is aware of the implied author's intention to amuse. Such a reader recognizes the overall humorous mode of the text, and she or he will have been cued into a pleasurable, playful frame of mind that facilitates amusement as a response to the text. As outlined previously, Triezenberg (2004, 2008) suggests that writers of comic fiction use devices called *humour enhancers* to ensure a humorous response to their works. Humour enhancers, which include broad classes such as *shared stereotypes*, are techniques which are not funny in themselves, but which signal to the reader that the text is supposed to be amusing. In this chapter, I explore the various types of stylistic devices (not discussed by Triezenberg) that, by stabilizing the narrative world as a humorous one, enhance the reader's humorous response.

3.2. *Stabilizing cues*: Creating a predisposition towards experiencing comedy

There are a number of ways in which the overall comicality of a text is established and negotiated between the writer, the text and the reader. This chapter outlines a range of techniques used by writers to signal their humorous intent, as well as some of the cognitive and affective states which are associated with readers' comprehension and experience of comedy. These comedy-inducing strategies and their effects are referred to as 'stabilising' with regard to creating comedy, meaning that they help to maintain a general impression that the text is a humorous one.

3.2.1. Mode versus mood

The humorous potential of comic narratives will be realized most successfully when appropriate textual devices have been used to cue the readers into both the *humorous mode* and the *humorous mood*, where the two are taken to mean the following:

> **Humorous mode**: (a) the larger comic frame of discourse that is (b) communicated by the sender of the text, and which (c) evokes a playful cognitive state that facilitates a humorous interpretation. It is the awareness that a text is amusing, which creates a cognitive expectation of comedy.
>
> **Humorous mood**: the pleasurable, low-intensity affective state that predisposes us towards experiencing the emotion of amusement. It is the feeling that a text is amusing, which creates an affective expectation of comedy.

These two states usually go hand-in-hand – the cognitive awareness influences the affective disposition, and vice versa. However, it is worth pointing out the distinction in order to explain the fact that it is possible to read or watch something that we know is intended to be funny and *not* be amused by it, that is, to be in the humorous mode, but not in the humorous mood. We are also likely to be amused by something that was not meant to be humorous when the humorous mood evoked by the text overrides the non-humorous mode for which it was intended. The latter situation can be seen in the following scene from Sue Townsend's *The Secret Diary of Adrian Mole, Aged 13¾*, where Adrian's father is cued into the wrong mood when watching a very serious, experimental, modern-day adaptation of the Nativity story performed by his son's class:

Example 2

Driving home in the car my father said, 'That was the funniest Nativity play I have ever seen. Whose idea was to turn it into a comedy?' I didn't reply. It wasn't a comedy.

(Townsend [1982] 2002: 215)

Even though the mode of the play was serious, Adrian's father had been cued into the humorous mood, presumably mistaking the unexpectedly severe, solemn elements of the narrative world for humorous cues. This affective state led him to form a cognitive impression of the mode of the text as a whole and confusing its actual intent. The (wrongly interpreted) emotional cues created an affective expectation which directed the humorous interpretation of the text.

The interpretation of a text can also be guided by a cognitive expectation regarding its humorous mode, that is, the awareness that what we read, hear or watch has been designed to be humorous. The importance of this kind of cognitive anticipation can be illustrated with the following example from Jerome K. Jerome's *Three Men in a Boat*, where, at a party, two young German men trick the protagonists into thinking that they are about to hear a comic song in German:

Example 3

'Oh, it will amuse you. You will laugh,' whispered the two young men, as they passed through the room, and took up an unobtrusive position behind the Professor's back.

Herr Slossenn Boschen accompanied himself. The prelude did not suggest a comic song exactly. It was a weird, soulful air. It quite made one's flesh creep; but we murmured to one another that it was the German method, and prepared to enjoy it.

(Jerome [1889] 1993: 73)

Not knowing any German, the English characters must rely on the explicit message ('Oh, it will amuse you. You will laugh.') and use it to prepare themselves for the enjoyable experience of comedy. Once in the humorous mode, they disregard all the other signals and laugh all the way through the performance – the performance of what later turns out to be one of the most tragic songs in the German language. 'If we had not known it was a funny song, we might have wept,' admits the protagonist even before the true meaning of the song has been explained to him (Jerome [1889] 1993: 74), thus illustrating the importance of anticipation in text comprehension.

The notions of cognitive and affective expectations with regard to experiencing narrative comedy can be compared with what Double (1997) defines as *faith*. With reference to stand-up comedy routines (which, unlike written narrative humour, Double describes as based predominantly on jokes), Double summarizes the 'secret formula' for a stand-up joke as: *Joke = Incongruity + Faith* (1997: 91). He suggests that while humorous incongruities on which jokes are based are relatively easy to think up, the challenge for a performer is: 'putting these incongruities across in a way which makes the audience believe they're actually funny, making them have faith that you really are a comedian and that it's OK to laugh' (Double 1997: 91).

Whether it is a stand-up routine, a play, a song or a novel, creating a humorous text requires not only putting together humorous material, but also cueing the receiver into thinking and feeling that the text is a humorous one. The very explicit cueing of the humorous mode in the

German song scene above was possible mostly due to the immediate nature of the live performance. The (misleading) meta-message 'this is comedy' was communicated to the audience members directly and unambiguously before the performance started, which would perhaps be difficult to imagine being exercised with written texts intended for solitary reading. That said, written texts such as novels or short stories can be subjected to an analogous type of cueing that directs the readers' expectations about the content even before the reading starts. The reader of *Three Men in a Boat*, for example, might have heard a variation on 'Oh, it will amuse you. You will laugh.' applied to the whole novel by means of personal recommendation from someone who had read it.

3.2.2. Paratexts

Aside from personal recommendation, another kind of explicit humorous cueing in written texts is that communicated through the *paratexts* (Genette 1997) which form the mediation between the reader, the author, the publisher and the book itself. Paratexts are those elements which are not part of the actual text, but which affect our impression of it even before the reading starts – this impression can start being formed as soon as we look at the cover of a book. For example, a quick glance at the blurb on the book's back cover should leave little doubt that *Three Men in a Boat* is 'perhaps the best-loved comic novel of the Victorian era' (Wordsworth Classics, 1993). With the covers of lesser-known books, these kinds of bold statements can be replaced by extracts from book reviews, purposefully cropped to communicate the most crucial information: the *Sunday Telegraph* review on the front cover of Haddon's *A Spot of Bother* has been condensed to 'Brilliant ... Very funny' (Vintage 2007) and *The Times* quote on Lewycka's *A Short History of Tractors in Ukrainian* simply says 'Extremely funny' (Penguin 2005). Some of the bestselling titles will combine reviews with an element of personal recommendation, ideally from an established comedy writer, such as Nick Hornby's testimonial, 'Helen Fielding is one of the funniest writers in Britain and Bridget Jones is a creation of comic genius' on the front of *Bridget Jones's Diary* (Picador 1998). Much like the young Germans' comment about the 'comic' song, these explicit statements found on book covers are early attempts at directing the receiver's cognitive expectations about the mode of the text. Readers' comments about the efficiency – and often misleading qualities – of these kinds of paratexts can be found in their online reviews of comic narratives. One Goodreads user, for example, writes:

> I picked up this book because it had rave reviews printed all over the back and inside covers about how hilarious it was. I don't know if I'm missing something but I didn't find this book funny at all.

The kinds of (sometimes misleading) recommendations and reviews to which the reader is referring are publishers' attempts to market the book as humorous, and as such they are largely external to – and sometimes completely beyond the control of – the author of the actual text. Writers of comic narratives, therefore, must find their own ways of ensuring appropriate framing for their work. It would perhaps not be appropriate for authors to proclaim their own books as 'creations of comic genius', and therefore the techniques used by them will be less explicit, allowing readers to guess the mode of the text rather than stating it directly. The comedian Spike Milligan's decision to call his Second World War memoirs *Adolf Hitler: My Part in His Downfall*, for example, is likely have been a conscious attempt at indicating the larger humorous mode of the autobiographical series. Even the most basic knowledge of history suffices to 'get' the joke – Milligan might have fought in the war, but the claim that he directly contributed to the 'downfall' (a word with rather grandiose connotations) of Adolf Hitler seems preposterous. The humorous incongruity between the wording of the title and the scale of what we suspect actually happened, as well as the amusing narcissism of it (narcissism and humour will be discussed further in the following chapter), may direct the reader's expectations as to the overall mode of the book. Milligan does not stop there, however, and continues this humorous cueing into the prologue:

Example 4

Prologue

After *Puckoon* I swore I would never write another novel. This is it …

(Milligan 1971: 11)

This brief and uninformative section appears to have little purpose rather than to cue a particular frame of mind in the reader. The paradox of holding in one's hands a novel which, technically, should not have been written, can result in a dissonance that is often thought to lie at the heart of humorous incongruity. Additionally, from Milligan 'swearing' that he would never write another novel we can infer that the writing of the previous one was not an experience that he was keen to repeat. Aside from creating a fleeting moment of amusement, this prologue also has wider implications for the way we approach the entire book. By suggesting that we are reading a novel which should not exist written by someone who did not particularly want to write it, Milligan is signalling his own tongue-in-cheek attitude towards the work, conveying a tone which can be described as ironic. The use of irony, defined as a perception of a conceptual paradox between two dimensions of the same event (Simpson 2011: 39), allows Milligan to introduce a humorous incongruity and set a humorous mode which stabilizes the reader's perception of the memoir as humorous.

Interestingly, Milligan's attempts to cue a humorous mode via the title and the prologue will, to some readers, be gratuitous. One Goodreads user's two-sentence-long review of *Adolf Hitler* reads simply:

It's Spike Milligan, isn't it. Of course it's funny.

Spike Milligan's fame as a comic writer and performer means that, to those readers familiar with his other work, just seeing his name on the cover of a book will act as a paratext which cues a humorous mode. Based on any previous experience of Spike Milligan's creations or even simply on basic knowledge of who he was, some readers may expect to be amused by a book written by him – and disappointed if the text does not deliver the expected humour. Together with the cover design, the book's title, and the prologue, the writer's name is therefore another example of a paratext which can stabilize the text as humorous.

3.2.3. Openings

While paratexts such as the cover design, the title, the prologue or even the author's name can help to start guiding our cognitive expectations about the mode of the text, it would be difficult to argue that, on their own, they significantly contribute to the creation of a particular mood. Complex evaluative states such as moods are products of combinations of textual cues that are spread throughout entire narratives and for that reason are not easy to 'pin down'. A useful starting point in the search of such cues, however, is the analysis of the opening sections of narratives, which establish the primary, dominant mood of the text in a way that minimizes the potential misinterpretation of what follows. Below is an outline of the main classes of stabilizing cues which help to establish our general impression of the narrative world as humorous. Even though the examples used here come from the openings of novels, all of those types of cues are also be used continuously throughout comic narratives.

(i) 'Humorous' humorous cues: Instances of humour

When it comes to introducing the reader to a humorous narrative world, it may seem like the most efficient and straightforward way of cueing an emotional orientation congruent with comedy would be to open with something that actually evokes amusement. An inherently humorous element such as a canned joke, a witticism or a one-liner based on a humorous incongruity, when placed in the opening, should evoke a brief moment of humorous emotion in the reader, a moment that would then trigger an overall comic mood. Even if the reader is not particularly amused by the joke, its mere occurrence could create awareness that we are reading a text that includes instances of humour, and so there would be a cognitive expectation of more to come. Milligan's *Adolf Hitler*, for example, is a novel which contains a high proportion of inherently funny quips, a quality that is signalled right from the beginning. The following paragraph follows from the previously discussed (and also inherently amusing) prologue:

Example 5

HOW IT ALL STARTED

September 3rd, 1939. The last minutes of peace ticking away. Father and I were watching Mother digging our air-raid shelter. (1) 'She's a great little woman,' said Father. 'And getting smaller all the time,' I added. Two minutes later, (2) a man called Chamberlain who did Prime Minister impressions spoke on the wireless; he said, 'As from eleven o'clock we are at war with Germany.' (3) (I loved the WE.) (4) 'War?' said Mother. 'It must have been something we said,' said Father. (5) The people next door panicked, burnt their post office books and took in the washing.

(Milligan 1971: 15, my numbering and underlining)

The lines underlined in this short passage are the ones which immediately stand out as humorous: a play on the non-literal meaning of the word 'little' as it is typically used in the phrase 'a great little woman' (1), a joke directed at the inefficiency of the wartime UK prime minister Neville Chamberlain (2), an ironic comment where the speaker says the opposite of what he thinks (3), a witty retort that downplays the seriousness of the subject (4), and an incongruous combination of activities presented as examples of wartime panic (5). These quips can be considered as signals of the overall mode of the text – a non-humorous narrative would be less likely to contain such abundance of inherently amusing elements than a humorous one. The one-liners can also be seen as cues of positive affect, since the brief episodes of amusement that they trigger can create an overall humorous mood and lead to a humour-congruent emotional predisposition towards experiencing more amusement.

One reason why this amusement-based method of cueing the humorous mood can be thought to be particularly effective is related to what Cantor, Bryant and Zillmann (1974) call *excitation transfer*. Excitation transfer is said to be a phenomenon where one's high level of excitation triggered by a rousing stimulus gets carried over and affects the perception of another stimulus. Cantor et al. conducted experiments in which subjects were cued into various degrees of both positive and negative emotional excitation, and then subsequently asked to rate the funniness of various jokes and cartoons. It was found that those people who were already in an excited state, regardless of whether the excitation was positive or negative, found the humorous materials more amusing than those in a state of low excitation. In the context of Example 5 above, it could be argued that the amusement triggered by such a high concentration of humorous lines in the opening raises the reader's excitation, thus positively affecting the perception of funniness in what follows. It may be relevant here that Spike Milligan was a performer as well as a writer, as this technique of evoking strong amusement in the introduction is not uncommon in stand-up comedy routines, in which, as comedian Stewart Lee points out, 'Received wisdom says, 'Open with your best line.'' (2010: 162). Opening with one's funniest line allows for the intense amusement evoked in the hearer/reader to be transferred into the following fragments of the text. What can be inferred from Lee's comment, however, is that even though the 'received wisdom' within the comedy-writing circles is that one should open with something particularly amusing, there are also other, perhaps more sophisticated, ways of establishing the humorous mood/mode at the start of a humorous text.

(ii) 'Non-humorous' humorous cues: Distancing and downgrading
The use of humorous material is certainly an effective way of cueing the humorous mode/mood, yet many writers will choose strategies which are less direct or explicit, but which can nevertheless guide the reader's expectations about the text. These strategies are not humorous in

themselves, but can help to establish a cognitive anticipation of comedy and a background affective state congruent with amusement:

Distancing: techniques aimed at increasing the reader's detachment from the narrative world in a way that helps him or her adopt a non-serious attitude about textual entities.

Downgrading: devices used to reduce the value or importance of elements of the narrative world to make it easier to perceive them as laughable.

(a) Distancing

The reason why distancing techniques can be particularly effective in cueing a humorous mode/mood can be explained with reference to *reversal theory*, which stipulates that humour is typically correlated with the metamotivational state called the *paratelic mode* (Apter 1982, 1991; see also Morreall 2009). Paratelic mode is a state in which real-life problems and goals are forgotten, and it is associated with various forms of play, where one's motivation is directed not towards achieving a goal, but with the pursuit of the activity itself. In the context of comic narratives, this humour-facilitating playful state of detachment from everyday concerns can be cued with the use of distancing techniques, which can help to establish a sense of a 'safe' distance from reality.

The first type of distancing used in comic narratives can be linked to the group of stylistic devices referred to as *foregrounding* (Havránek and Mukařovský in Garvin's 1964 translation, see also van Peer 1986; van Peer and Hakemulder 2006), meaning those techniques which allow the writer to draw the reader's attention to the stylistic layer of the work. Such a shift of focus to the usually backgrounded linguistic level of the text can lead to language becoming *defamiliarized* (Shklovsky [1917] 1965), as we are encouraged to look at familiar words and expressions in new, unexpected ways. As far as cueing a humorous mode/mood is concerned, foregrounding can be effective in shifting our attention from the narrative world events to the stylistic level of the text, thus distancing us from the events themselves. With regard to humour creation, it can be said to help communicate the meta-message 'this is play' (Bateson 2006), crucial in establishing the cognitive anticipation of a playful activity and triggering a switch to the paratelic mode of comprehension. The following, foregrounding-dense opening of Joseph Heller's *Catch-22* may not be inherently amusing, but can nevertheless trigger a non-serious frame of interpretation:

Example 6

Yossarian was in the hospital with a pain in his liver that fell just short of being jaundice. The doctors were puzzled by the fact that it wasn't quite jaundice. If it became jaundice they could treat it. If it didn't become jaundice and went away they could discharge him. But this just being short of jaundice all the time confused them.

(Heller 1994: 7)

The foregrounding technique used here is the seemingly redundant repetition of the word 'jaundice'. This kind of lexical repetition can be linked to what van Peer, in his discussion of foregrounding (1986), calls *parallelism*: a process 'in which the author has repeatedly made the same, or similar, choices where the normal flux of language would tend to variation in selection' (van Peer 1986: 23, see also van Peer and Hakemulder 2006: 547). By putting so much emphasis on the word 'jaundice', the narrator shifts some of the focus from the actual illness in its narrative world context to the playful exploration of the lexical term in the stylistic layer of the text. This partial shift of focus from the narrative events to the language of the narrative thus distances us from the narrative world – by foregrounding the literariness and the make-believe nature of the narrative, it facilitates a detached, paratelic mode of comprehension by reiterating the meta-message 'this is play'.

A different form of distancing found in comic narratives is that which draws our attention not to the stylistic level of the text, but to the act of storytelling itself. *Metafictional distance*, according to Vandelanotte (2010), is that in which the narrator distances him- or herself from the narrative, exposing and disrupting the functioning of the narrative world. An example of this can be seen in the opening of P.G. Wodehouse's *Right Ho, Jeeves*:

Example 7

'Jeeves,' I said, 'may I speak frankly?'
  'Certainly, sir.'
  'What I have to say may wound you.'
  'Not at all, sir.'
  'Well, then –'
  No – wait. Hold the line a minute. I've gone off the rails.

I don't know if you have had the same experience, but the snag I always come up against when I'm telling a story is this dashed difficult problem of where to begin it. It's a thing you don't want to go wrong over, because one false step and you're sunk. I mean, if you fool about too long at the start, trying to establish atmosphere, as they call it, and all that sort of rot, you fail to grip and the customers walk out on you.
(Wodehouse 2008: 9)

Wodehouse's narrator asks the reader to 'wait' and 'hold the line' as he temporarily disrupts the flow of the narrative in order to share his doubts about setting the right atmosphere when beginning a story. By referring to the act of narrating itself, the author emphasizes the fictionality of the text, thus distancing the reader from the content, implying perhaps that we do not need to take this story very seriously, because it is just a piece of writing. This kind of distancing can cue us into a detached paratelic mode more explicitly than the foregrounding discussed above – here, it is not the individual lexical choices which are brought to our attention, but the fictional, made-up nature of the text itself.

Distancing techniques can be used to shift our attention to the literariness or fictionality of the text, thus disassociating us from narrative world events. Not all distancing devices will be related to increasing metalinguistic or metafictional distance, however. Some distancing techniques found in humorous openings will be associated with the point of view that the reader is led to adopt when reading the text. As will be shown further in this chapter, a distanced perspective which facilitates the humorous mode/mood can also be achieved by decreasing the levels of sensory or emotional detail surrounding narrative world events, or by using the point of view of a character who has a detached attitude about those events.

(b) *Downgrading*
As far as literary texts are concerned, a distanced attitude (and the distancing techniques which trigger it) are not specific to comedy, as any form of ludic reading can generally be considered to require a switch to the detached, paratelic state associated with play. That is why the addition of downgrading devices may be particularly useful in cueing a specifically humorous mode/mood in comic narratives. In reversal theory terms, downgrading has been described as an excitation-inducing *cognitive synergy* (meaning a combination of multiple incongruous characteristics under a single identity, e.g. Murgatroyd 1985), which can sometimes have an amusing effect. Apter (1982) suggests that downgrading of threatening identities (e.g. bosses) can be a particularly humorous type of synergy that combines the intimidating with the inconsequential. This kind of downgrading of an identity, apart from being inherently incongruous, gains its further humorous potential from the way in which it allows us to laugh *at* that identity – a quality emphasized by those theories of humour concerned with aggression towards and superiority over the humorous object. Downgrading techniques, then, can complement the distancing ones in cueing a mode that is not only playful, but even specifically humorous. By imbuing textual entities with unexpectedly belittling, unflattering qualities, downgrading devices provide the reader with the perception of incongruity and the feeling of superiority which are often thought to lie at the heart of humour.

Some downgrading techniques are used to *deprecate*, that is, to disparage or express disapproval of textual entities in a way which potentially increases the reader's sense of superiority over the downgraded object. The following example from the opening of David Sedaris' autobiographical short story 'The Learning Curve' is interesting in that the narrator is making the object of humour out of himself by being self-deprecating for comic purposes:

Example 8

After my graduation from the School of Art Institute of Chicago, a terrible mistake was made and I was offered a position teaching a writing workshop. I had never gone to graduate school, and although several of my stories had been Xeroxed and stapled, none of them had ever been published in the traditional sense of the word.

(Sedaris 2002: 83)

Using explicitly deprecating techniques at the beginning of the story – like the narrator's references to his own lack of success as a writer – predisposes the reader to be amused at the narrator's cost. By putting himself down, the narrator is allowing the reader to feel superior, which can facilitate a humorous response. The actual humorous potential of the opening, however, is most likely to lie in the internal incongruity between the two clauses in the sentence 'a terrible mistake was made and I was offered a position teaching a writing workshop'. In line with the classic incongruity-resolution approach to humour appreciation (Suls 1972) the first clause can be said to set a certain expectation as to what will follow, which is then surprisingly disrupted by the ill-fitting ending. The incongruity between the negative first clause and the unexpectedly positive second one is resolved when we realize that the narrator is humorously downgrading his own skills and qualifications. This particular example of self-deprecation shows how humour-inducing superiority and incongruity can be combined through downgrading techniques.

While deprecating downgrading devices are concerned with disparaging textual entities, other downgrading strategies are used to reduce the importance, gravity or formality of elements which could otherwise seem too serious to be taken humorously. This kind of *downplaying* can indicate that the narrative world is not an entirely serious one, and that it is acceptable to be amused by it. In the opening of Marina Lewycka's *A Short History of Tractors in Ukrainian*, the author slightly downplays the usually more dignified concept of 'family ghosts':

Example 9

Two years after my mother died, my father fell in love with a glamorous blonde Ukrainian divorceé. He was eighty-four and she was thirty-six. She exploded into our lives like a fluffy pink grenade, churning up the murky water, bringing to the surface a sludge of sloughed-off memories, giving the family ghosts a kick up the backside.

(Lewycka 2005: 1)

Family ghosts here are, rather surprisingly, being given 'a kick up the backside'. This expression does not seem directed at disparaging them, as the ghosts themselves are not described in any disapproving terms. Presenting the ghosts as having a 'backside', however, grounds them in the 'real', recognizable world of human experience, thus reducing their ethereal intangibility. Such downplaying of the normally unearthly, transcendental subject of family ghosts can signal to the reader that some of the other serious topics in the novel will be approached with a dose of flippancy.

3.3. *Destabilizing cues*: Disrupting expectations within the humorous context

The experience of humour is typically associated with the positive emotion of amusement. The relationship between amusement and other affective states is rather ambiguous, however, as it has been claimed that the detached perspective necessary for amusement distances us from experiencing any other emotions; Bergson, for example, argued that laughter is incompatible with emotion, as comedy appeals exclusively to intelligence (1913). In what follows, I show how, rather than inhibiting non-humorous affective states, comic narratives are in fact constructed to evoke a range of moods and emotions, some of which are far from positive and do not seem to be compatible with the disengaged, light-hearted, non-serious humorous responses. The existence of such combinations of amusement and other emotions, here referred to as *complex humorous responses*, helps to explain why, despite the positive emotional associations of comedy, book covers of humorous novels can still be labelled with the following mixes of terms:

> 'Delightful, funny, touching' Spectator (*A Short History of Tractors in Ukrainian*, Penguin 2006)
>
> 'A painful, funny, humane novel' *The Times* (*A Spot of Bother*, Vintage 2007)

Interestingly, these quotes have been placed on the *back* covers of the novels – the reviews on their front covers present these books as 'funny' above everything else, suggesting perhaps that the publishers intended for the texts to be regarded primarily as comedies. Neither of these books, however, can be considered amusing to the extent that they inhibit the reader from experiencing moments of serious thought and negative emotion. While they may rely on cueing the humorous mode/mood in order to stabilize comedy, they also destabilize it by introducing elements which are non-humorous, and which therefore create an impression of amusement *combined with* 'touching' or 'painful' emotion.

The reader will occasionally be alerted to these emotional combinations through paratexts (like the quotes discussed above), but, as in the case of cueing a humorous mode/mood, the signals will often appear in the opening of the actual text as well. In *A Spot of Bother* – a novel which, as I mentioned previously, has been described as 'heartbreaking and funny' by one of its readers – Mark Haddon introduces the narrative world with the following passage:

Example 10

> It began when George was trying on a black suit in Allders the week before Bob Green's funeral.
>
> It was not the prospect of the funeral that had unsettled him. Nor Bob dying. To be honest he had always found Bob's locker-room

bonhomie slightly tiring and he was secretly relieved that they would not be playing squash again. Moreover, the manner in which Bob had died (a heart attack while watching the Boat Race on television) was oddly reassuring. Susan had come back from her sister's and found him lying on his back in the centre of the room with one hand over his eyes, looking so peaceful she thought initially that he was taking a nap.

(Haddon 2007: 1)

This opening, whether or not it evokes amusement, contains distancing and downgrading elements which can potentially cue a non-serious, detached mode of comprehension in the reader, especially considering the subject matter. Although the extract deals primarily with death, the reader is not encouraged to respond to the (typically tragic) event in an engaged, heartfelt manner – rather, we adopt the detached point of view of the main character, who admits not only to not being unsettled by his acquaintance's death, but also to being 'secretly relieved' about it. Aside from distancing the reader from the emotional weight of the situation, George's relief – and especially the accompanying description of his former squash partner's tiring locker-room manner – can be viewed as a downgrading strategy which slightly deprecates Bob and downplays the gravity of his death. The event of death itself is additionally portrayed in a rather undramatic way ('a heart attack while watching the Boat Race on television'), a manner which George finds 'oddly reassuring'. The techniques which, in the opening extract, distance us from the weight of the difficult subject matter and downgrade its seriousness can suggest to the reader that the approach to death and other difficult themes in *A Spot of Bother* may occasionally border on flippant. Importantly, however, the fact that a description of someone's death is used to introduce us to the entire narrative world signals that such serious, not transparently funny subjects will play a significant part in this otherwise amusing novel.

The serious subjects which occur in comic narratives (such as the death in the passage above) will here be referred to as *dark elements*. The linguistic expression of such dark elements can be explained with reference to the cognitive stylistic applications of *schema theory*. Schema theory originated in psychology as an aspect of Bartlett's ([1932] 1995) theory of remembering, where the mechanism of adult human remembering was said to rely on an individual's assortment of *schemata* coordinated and organized according to the attitudes, interests and ideals which build them up ([1932] 1995: 308). 'Schema,' in Bartlett's theory, 'refers to an active organisation of past reactions, or of past experiences, which must always be supposed to be operating in any well-adapted organic response' (Bartlett [1932] 1995: 201). This psychological concept of schemata as organizations of built-up memories which shape our reactions to the environment was subsequently used at the intersection of text processing and artificial intelligence, where schemata were seen as 'the building blocks of cognition' which allow readers to understand written texts (e.g. Rumelhart 1980). Schemata, from that perspective, can be defined as the mental stores of information which form the background knowledge about the world that we rely on when processing discourse (see Emmott, Alexander and Marszalek 2014 for stylistic applications of schema theory).

Schema theory, although useful in making basic assumptions about discourse comprehension, makes little reference to the emotional weight carried by particular schemata – a limitation emphasized by Semino (1997: 149–51) in her discussion of the theory's application to literary linguistic analysis. In her own account of literary texts, however, Semino does consider 'the likely emotional associations of different schemata' – an idea based on existing research in the emotional states (positive, negative, neutral, or a combination) typically associated with culture-specific knowledge about various circumstances and situations (1997: 151, based on Conway and Bekerian 1987 and Lehnert and Vine 1987). The necessity to complement the purely cognitive concept of a schema with an evaluative component of – positive or negative – affect is also discussed by van Dijk (e.g. 1989), who uses the term *attitude schemata* to explain how our social memory can store positive and negative attitudes towards particular social groups. A similar approach is proposed by Montoro (2007), whose concept of *positive affective schemas* explains the positive attitudes evoked in readers as a response to certain fictional characters (the relationship between affect and social cognition will be discussed further in the following chapter).

3.3.1. Switching to a non-humorous mood

Some comic narratives deal with extremely 'non-humorous' subjects such as death, illness or war. While there will be times when such elements are used for a humorous effect, sometimes the authors will choose to suspend the overall humorous mood and allow these dark elements to trigger highly serious and unpleasant emotional states. In those cases, even if the background mood has been established as humorous, a dark element can trigger a shift to a non-humorous one, accompanied by moments of acute negative emotion.

Clear examples of such extreme mood shifts can be seen in *A Short History of Tractors in Ukrainian*, where the main, generally humorous, narrative set in present-day England is occasionally interrupted by deeply disturbing flashbacks from early-twentieth-century Eastern Europe. The novel can be said to be built around a number of conceptual spaces, or *text worlds* (Werth 1999), where the reader is required to switch between the main, present-day, England-based world inhabited by Nadia (the first-person narrator of Ukrainian parentage born and raised in England after the war) and the intermittent mainland European wartime worlds, from which Nadia is absent. *World-switches*, according to Gavins, occur when the temporal boundaries of a text-world shift and readers are led to construct new text worlds with distinct time-zones (Gavins 2007: 48). In the case of *A Short History*, the text worlds differ not only temporally, but also spatially and, most importantly here, *emotionally*, as they evoke very distinct moods. This quality of the novel has been commented on by one Goodreads user, who points out that:

> This story is so neatly balanced between the humour and farce of the present 'situation' and the scary, desperate past.

In Example 11, which illustrates this point, Nadia and her sister Vera are chatting while getting ready for bed in Nadia's house in Peterborough, England. Their jokey exchange about their dad (which corresponds with the overall humorous mood of world-1, the main text world) gradually leads to a switch to a very different world, world-2, where the mood changes completely. There distinction between the two worlds is very clear – the switch between present-day Peterborough and wartime Drachensee is explicitly marked by the graphic boundary '***'. The switch itself, however, is not entirely abrupt, as it is mediated by a *buffer* section, where Nadia and Vera negotiate whether the switch should be brought about or not.

Example 11

(**world-1 starts**) 'Surely he couldn't be *so* stupid.'

'Of course he could,' says Vera. 'Look at his track record so far.'

We chuckle smugly. I feel close to her and far at the same time, stacked up above her in the dark. When we were children we used to share jokes about our parents.

[**buffer starts**] It must be at least three o'clock in the morning. […] I know there may never be a chance like this again.

'Pappa said something happened to you in the camp at Drachensee. Something about cigarettes. Do you remember?'

'Of course I remember.' I wait for her to continue, and after a while she says, 'There are some things it's better not to know, Nadia.'

'I know. But tell me anyway.' [**buffer ends**] (**world-1 ends**)

* * *

(**world-2 starts**) The labour camp at Drachensee was a huge, ugly, chaotic and cruel place. […]

(Lewycka 2005: 268, my bold and brackets)

Vera, who experienced the reality of the Drachensee world as a child, is not keen to relive the memories for the benefit of her sister. Her reluctance cues the reader in the external *discourse world* (Werth 1999) that the switch will not be a pleasant one and that we should prepare ourselves for a radical shift of mood in the new world. As it can be seen in the passage below (Example 12), the world of the concentration camp where Vera and her parents were detained is an entirely non-humorous world. Interestingly, the extract contains phrases and passages that can be linked to the distancing and downgrading techniques which, in a humorous world, would be associated with signalling a humorous mode/mood and stabilizing comedy. In this particular world, however, humorous cueing is suspended due to a change in mode and mood:

Example 12

The labour camp at Drachensee was a huge, ugly, chaotic and cruel place. Forced labourers from Poland, Ukraine, Belarus, conscripted to boost the German war effort, communists and trade unionists sent from the Low Countries for re-education, Gypsies, homosexuals, criminals, Jews in transit to their deaths, inmates of lunatic asylums and captured resistance fighters, all lived cheek by jowl in low concrete lice-infested barracks. In such a place, the only order was terror. And the rule of terror was reinforced at every level; each community and subcommunity had its own hierarchy of terror.

(Lewycka 2005: 268–9)

This expository paragraph leads us, potentially, to anticipate distressing events to follow further in the narrative. The highly negative emotional impact of the setting is rooted largely in its perceived realism – we are aware that the construction of this largely fictional labour camp world must have been based on the author's research into a particularly tragic period of modern history. The mere mention of the introductory phrase 'the labour camp at Drachensee', therefore, may have a destabilizing effect on the reader's mood. The perceived authenticity of this hopeless world so rigidly separated from the main, humorous, text world of the novel means that the distancing and deprecating stylistic techniques used in the passage lose the comic potential which they could be expected to trigger in a humorous context. Previously, I showed how the deprecation of textual entities can be linked to establishing a humorous mood. Here, the camp is described as 'ugly, chaotic and cruel', but the effect is far from amusing. Similarly, the extensive list of types of detainees confined in a sentence that is uncharacteristically long for the style of the novel, and the repetition of the word 'terror' in the final lines could be seen as foregrounding techniques which draw attention to the style of the text and distance us from the events described. Again, their occurrence here adds to the threatening mood, not a humorous one.

It would be easy to assume that these distancing and downgrading techniques do not have the same effect here as they did in the humorous openings because the subject matter is so tragic that it completely inhibits our humorous response. As will be shown further, however, similarly disturbing and equally realistic elements can appear in humorous narrative worlds and have rather more amusing effects. The difference is in the implied author/narrator giving us *permission to laugh*. 'Permission to laugh' is a term which comedian Stewart Lee (2010) uses to explain how audiences can be manipulated to laugh at something that they find uncomfortable. For Lee, permission to laugh is something that can be granted by a comedian through particular combinations of structural devices built into the comic text – it is a stylistic manipulation of the receivers' interpretation of the text that is part of 'the comedy process' (2010: 213). In more theoretical, socio-culturally oriented approaches to humour, *permissibility* of certain jokes is sometimes thought of as a quality that is determined by the sociocultural situation – the nature of the occasion, the relationship between the participants and the cultural and historical factors will all have an impact on whether a particular joke is successful or not (Douglas 1968; Palmer 1994; Ermida 2009).

Writers of comic narratives have an ability to grant the reader permission to laugh at humour that would not otherwise be permissible. It was shown above that in the main text world of *A Short History*, the reader is encouraged to interpret events playfully and to anticipate amusement as an appropriate response – permission to laugh is granted. In the sub-world of the concentration camp, however, this permission is denied, as the reader is cued into a serious mode/mood and comedy is destabilized. In Example 11, Marina Lewycka achieves this by overtly, physically separating the non-humorous world from the main, humorous text world. This can be contrasted with the approach taken by Spike Milligan in *Adolf Hitler*, whose primary text world is set in wartime Britain. In Example 13 below, Milligan can be seen to cue a mood shift while at the same time granting us permission to laugh at a disturbing situation. In the final paragraph of the last chapter of the memoir, which follows Milligan's army training in England, the protagonist is making himself comfortable on a ship which is finally about to take him from Liverpool to Algiers, where the fighting will start:

Example 13

(world-1 starts) I set about putting up my hammock. It was very easy and I vaulted in like an old salt. No, I didn't fall out. Sorry. [**buffer starts**] In the dark, I smoked a cigarette, and thought … [**buffer ends**] **(world-2 starts)** We were going to war. Would I survive? Would I be frightened? Could I survive a direct hit at point blank range by a German 88 mm.? Could I really push a bayonet into a man's body – twist it – and pull it out? I mean what would the neighbours say?
(world-2 ends) (world-1 ends)

(Milligan 1971: 133, my bold and brackets)

The sentence which stands out here is the final line 'I mean what would the neighbours say?' – even though the entire memoir is packed with similar quips, the jokey line suddenly seems inappropriate in the context. That is because the mood has been switched to serious as the narrator stops joking about hammocks and suddenly explicitly alerts the reader to the severity of the situation. The shift, although quicker than in the *A Short History* example above (Example 11), has been conducted with the use of similar techniques, that is, a world-switch preceded by a buffering element. The line 'In the dark, I smoked a cigarette, and thought …' can be considered a buffer which mediates the transition between world-1, the humorous text world of the ship, to world-2, the serious world of the narrator's imagined future. The latter world can be classified as a *sub-world* (Werth 1999), as it exists within the main text world and is dependent on the participants of that higher-level world. What is interesting here is that the seriousness of the sub-world is disrupted by the final, humorous, line. Unlike in Example 11, the distinction between the two worlds is not as clear-cut: seriousness is not only contained within the larger humorous world, but it contains humorous elements itself. Although the mood shift is evident, a lack of a clear boundary can help us infer that laughter is still permitted within the serious world, and so the overall humorous mode/mood of the book is not overturned. This strategy, as illustrated by one of the Goodreads reviews of the memoir, can be seen as inappropriate by some readers:

> I didn't like this book.
>
> WW2 was not a joke and this book makes the armed forces look like a bunch of bumbling idiots. I really have to wonder how 'Spike' made it out alive.

The lack of clear boundaries between the serious and the humorous in Milligan's text means that the serious, negatively charged world of the Second World War is usually presented in the humorous mode – a portrayal that some readers may find offensive and disrespectful, as it trivializes the subject matter which, in the view of those readers, should be retained in the serious mode.

3.3.2. Enhancing the humorous mood

While some comic narratives employ dark elements in order to shift the mood, often as a way of introducing a more serious topic, others use them specifically for humour creation. The way in which amusement can be brought out of elements which would normally be expected to evoke negative emotion can be associated with is referred to as *dark humour* (see e.g. Bloom 2010), *black humour* (Friedman 1969) or *gallows humour* (Obrdlik 1942). In his cognitive poetic account of black jokes, Tsur (1989) suggests that this type of humour results from an 'extreme shifts of mental sets', where receivers are led to switch from an innocuous script to an unpleasant or shocking one. The following example from *A Spot of Bother* contains this type of humorous one-liner which involves two incompatible scripts, one of which is tragic:

Example 14
He remembered his own thirtieth wedding anniversary. Bob staggering across the lawn, slapping a drunken arm around his shoulder and saying, 'The funny thing is, if you'd killed her you'd have been out by now.'
(Haddon 2007: 60)

The joke relies on the juxtaposition of the 'marriage' script with the 'murder' script, which leads us to make comparisons between thirty years of married life and thirty years of imprisonment, the latter presented as leading to a more positive outcome. The simple humour-bearing script opposition is enhanced by an extreme shift of mental sets, which happens as a result of incorporating the highly negative 'murder' script into a humorous framework. The joke relies on its own internal humorous incongruity, which makes it funny out of context. However, these types of inherently amusing jokes are rare in comic novels and short stories, and so writers of comedy will have to use different stylistic strategies to turn 'unfunny' into funny.

(i)   Dark humour as an incongruity between the dark and the light
Many linguistic approaches to verbal humour describe an incongruity between contrasting concepts as the main source of humour. The following example from David Sedaris' short story 'Jesus Shaves' illustrates how serious, dark elements, when juxtaposed with more trivial ones, can help to create humour:

Example 15
In the evening we had the traditional Greek meal followed by a game in which we would toast one another with blood-colored eggs. The symbolism escapes me, but the holder of the table's one uncracked egg was supposedly rewarded with a year of good luck. I won only once. It was the year my mother died, my apartment got broken into, and I was taken to the emergency room suffering from what the attending physician diagnosed as 'housewife's knee'.
(Sedaris 2002: 176–7)

With regard to the traditional, script-based approach to humour (Raskin 1985), this passage can be said to be built around two incompatible scripts: 'good luck' and 'bad luck'. The positive opening leads us to formulate a 'good luck' script, and the expectation that follows from 'I won only once.' is unexpectedly violated by the list of events which evoke a 'bad luck' script. The disparity between the emotional weight of the two can lead to what Tsur (as outlined above) calls an extreme mental shift, where the reader resolves the incongruity between 'good' and 'bad' luck to conclude that the Greek egg tradition is not entirely credible. What is notable is that this main incongruity is enhanced by another, embedded, incongruity in the second part of the passage: 'It was the year my mother died, my apartment got broken into, and I was taken to the emergency room suffering from what the attending physician diagnosed as "housewife's knee."' (Sedaris 2002: 177). Taken out of context, this surprising ending can be seen to retain some of its humour, as it is built on its own internal humorous incongruity. The final element in the list of three tragic life events can be said to stand out from the rest, partly because it is contained within a sentence which is considerably longer than the other two, and partly because of the nature of the situation. Apart from the humorous incongruity potentially arising from the fact that the sufferer of 'housewife's knee' is a man, the choice of the folk, non-Latinate term used to describe the injury reduces the gravity of the situation. In the list of events presented, 'mother's death', 'apartment break-in' and 'housewife's knee', the latter leads to surprise, as it does not exactly match the seriousness of the first two.

The fact that these events are presented in the form of a list of three only enhances the humorous potential of the passage. Lists are especially useful for comic purposes in that they can provide a comic build-up which leads to what, in a canned joke, would be called a 'punch line'. In the account of his own comedy writing, Stewart Lee outlines how a *list of three things* – a device often used by stand-up comedians – relies on two elements followed by one that raises a laugh, a 'topper' (2010: 64). The first two provide the build-up, which is subsequently discharged. Lee does not elaborate on how to best choose these three elements in order to ensure humour – in fact, he suggests that 'this is almost alchemical, beyond reason' (2010: 66). As shown above, the humorous effect of the 'list of three' device can be linked to the incongruous nature of the final element. It can be seen, therefore, that one of the ways in which lists help to bring humour out of dark elements is to create incongruity by juxtaposing negative events with differing levels of severity. A case of 'housewife's knee', although undoubtedly distressing for the patient, appears trivial when contrasted with the much more serious events of 'mother's death' and 'apartment break-in'. The potential triviality is likely to be interpreted as humorous when the non-serious element appears in the 'punch line' slot, that is, at the end of the sequence.

(ii) Dark humour as an exaggeration of the dark

While humorous lists of three sometimes rely on unexpected juxtapositions of items, some lists of dark elements found in comic narratives will help to create humour not only through the combination of the types of elements involved, but also through the number of them. In an otherwise humorous context, amplification of negatively charged dark elements can be linked to what is commonly viewed as 'exaggeration for comic effect' – a technique related to what Nash (1985: 169) describes as the conventional comic tropes of *overstatement* and *hyperbole*. In the example below, the form of a list allows for a comic build-up as well as an opportunity to exaggerate for humour purposes:

Example 16

'Apparently, going on holiday is the fourth most stressful thing you can do,' said Katie. 'After the death of a spouse and changing your job. If I remember correctly.'
    'Fourth?' Ray said, staring at the water. 'What about if your kid dies?'
    'OK. Maybe not the fourth.'
    'Wife dies. Kid with disability,' said Ray.
    'Terminal disease,' said Katie. 'Loss of limb. Car crash.'
    'House burning down,' said Ray.
    'Declaration of war,' said Katie.

'Seeing a dog run over.'
'Seeing a person run over.'
'Actually running a person over,' said Ray.
'Actually running a dog over.'
'Running an entire family over.'
They were laughing again.

(Haddon 2007: 252)

This conversation, which is essentially a list of very tragic life events, leads to the characters' (and possibly also the reader's) amusement. The distancing effect of this hypothetical, impersonal list is enhanced by the internal incongruity between the types of dark elements which appear in it ('seeing a dog run over' may seem surprisingly trivial when it follows straight from 'declaration of war'). The humorous potential is also increased by the gradual build-up which leads up to a punch line-like final entry that triggers Katie and Ray's laughter. Interestingly, unlike in the 'housewife's knee' example above, the punch line here ('running an entire family over') is not an element of the least emotional weight, but one which is highly negative. In fact, it is so negative that it appears excessive and improbable. It is not only the final entry in the list which is exaggerated, however. The purpose of the whole exchange between Katie and Ray seems to be to 'top' the tragic event contrived by the previous speaker. This level of excess means that while each individual element on the list is negatively charged, en masse, they appear too fabricated to be taken seriously. Exaggeration, then, can be seen as a form of distancing the reader from the depicted events in a way which may bring about permission to laugh.

(iii) Dark humour as an exaggerated incongruity

To achieve humorous effects, non-humorous, dark elements can either be incongruously placed in contrast to less-serious ones or absurdly exaggerated. The two techniques of exaggeration and contrast are especially effective when combined. This combination can simply be achieved within an extended list of dark elements of varying emotional charge, as in Example 16. It can, however, be more subtle than that.

A powerful device for narrative humour creation which involves this kind of manipulation of dark elements is to present an objectively trivial situation in an over-the-top negative way. Playing something non-serious up as excessively serious is a source of humorous incongruity enhanced by humorous exaggeration. In Example 17 below, the narrator of Sedaris' 'Me Talk Pretty One Day' is describing his 'traumatic' experiences (due to a rude, unpleasant teacher) in a French language school:

Example 17

My only comfort was the knowledge that I was not alone. Huddled in the hallways and making the most of our pathetic French, my fellow students and I engaged in the sort of conversation commonly overheard in refugee camps.

'Sometimes me cry alone at night.'

'That be common for I, also, but be more strong, you. Much work and someday you talk pretty. People start love you soon. Maybe tomorrow, okay.'

(Sedaris 2002: 172)

Regardless of the actual nature of the French language school, comparing it to a refugee camp stands out in two ways. Firstly, a 'language school' and a 'refugee camp', even though both associated with temporary assemblages of strangers, are very different in the level of negative emotional impact associated with them. Describing a language school in terms of a refugee camp is a source of humorous incongruity – humorous, because the surprising incongruity is resolved once we recognize that the actual, non-serious situation has been blown out of proportion.

3.3.3. Blending the humorous and the non-humorous

Dark elements can affect our experience of humorous narrative worlds by temporarily shifting the mood to a more serious one, or alternatively, by enhancing the humorous mood by creating dark humour. These techniques, although they were said to evoke contrasting emotional responses (negative emotion versus amusement), can nevertheless be seen to be linked to the idea of complex humorous responses, as they rely on destabilizing, negatively charged elements being introduced to worlds which are otherwise stabilized as largely positive. Importantly, however, in an otherwise humorous world, the balance of moods will not be significantly affected by the occurrence of dark elements – despite the introduction of destabilizing cues, the generally humorous *primary mood* will be preserved. 'Primary mood' is a term used by Smith (2003), who argues that in films classified as *genre blends*, which rely on mixes of various mood cues (e.g. comedy horrors), the primary mood will not be overturned as long as the secondary cues are kept fairly brief (2003: 51). King (2002), similarly, also refers to this idea of a balance of moods (or *tones*, as he calls them), suggesting that while in some films comedy will be allowed to dominate the general tone, in others it will simply provide moments of relief or disruption in an otherwise non-humorous context.

This book is focused on those narratives in which the primary humorous mood dominates the overall ambience of the text. It does not, however, ignore the importance of the secondary moods evoked by writers, as those are believed to significantly contribute to our experience of narrative worlds. In fact, one of the reasons why some of the texts analysed here will not be equally amusing to all readers (as illustrated by some of the Goodreads comments throughout) is that some of us will be so highly affected by the secondary non-humorous moods evoked that our experience of the humorous mood will be compromised. An example of this is Lewycka's *A Short History of Tractors in Ukrainian*: a winner of the Bollinger Everyman Wodehouse Prize for comic fiction, and yet a book so tragic in its descriptions of wartime Europe, that some readers, as can be inferred from the Goodreads reviews discussed previously, would not be likely to classify it as a comedy. The overall balance of moods can affect our impression of the text, but it can also directly impact on our experience of the individual elements of humorous narrative worlds.

Many comic narratives include instances where the humorous and non-humorous moods are not as much experienced alongside each other, as they are blended into one, complex, contradictory mood. The use of serious or negative elements in a humorous context, aside from shifting the mood or enhancing it, can lead to a much more complex response, where amusement and other emotions are experienced simultaneously. In his account of film comedy, King (2002: 196) sums up this quality of blending comedy and seriousness, suggesting that such a mix 'results in something more than a simple sum of the parts' and 'generates, potentially, a state of unstable and contradictory emotional response'. Cueing this contradictory emotional response is a balancing act between maintaining two conflicting states: the detached, non-serious, playful frame of mind which facilitates amusement, and the engaged, heartfelt mood which opens us up to experiencing other narrative emotions. This dichotomy is explicitly laid out in King's (2011) analysis of the dark comedy *In Bruges* (dir. Martin McDonagh, 2008): a film which, according to King (2011: 133), combines humorous irony/detachment with more conventional/mainstream emotional engagement. King suggests that the humorous detachment can be cued through the devices of *irony*, *incongruity* and *reflexivity*, where reflexivity means self-referential elements that foreground the role of the producer of the text. The consequent detachment not only facilitates humour, but also acts as a 'defensive layer' which 'insulates' the viewer from the often painful, emotionally disturbing events in the narrative world (King 2011: 143). This insulation of detachment, however, is only partial, as the film manages to simultaneously encourage us to closely engage with the fates and feelings of its characters.

One reason why *In Bruges* is successful in blending the detached humorous with the closely engaged non-humorous is that its plot, even though stylistically manipulated to increase humorous distance, revolves around highly dramatic events which happen to very sympathetic characters. Since characters and story events will be elaborated on in the following chapters, here I focus on the relative emotional weight of the schemata that contribute to the complex humorous responses in those comedies which blend the serious with the trivial. The plot of *In Bruges*, for example, is based on elements such as murder, suicide, extreme violence, drug overuse, injury/mutilation and racial tensions – strongly negatively charged schemata which, even individually (let alone all together), could be expected to lead to destabilizing effects in any comedy. The apparent seriousness of the emotional charge of these schemata is key to the power of the mood blends which they provoke.

I showed previously that serious, dark elements can become humorous if their seriousness is incongruously exaggerated, or 'played up'. Here, I suggest that elements which are inherently serious, when 'played down' to appear more trivial with the use of distancing or downgrading techniques, are able to retain their emotional charge while simultaneously triggering amusement. Some of the most clear-cut examples of mood blends leading to complex humorous responses are those evoked by particularly serious elements whose seriousness has been played down for comic effect. An interesting item for the purpose of this kind of investigation is 'death of a relative', which, despite its painful, serious associations, can be successfully used for humour creation. Stylistic manipulations – particularly those of narrative distance – used to depict the death of a relative can potentially lead to a number of reactions, ranging from straightforward amusement to complex, contradictory mixes of emotions. The following extract from Douglas Adams' *The Hitchhiker's Guide to the Galaxy* is an example of how a mention of a death of a relative can be manipulated to become a source of humour, thus stabilizing our experience of comedy. It is part of a footnote which elaborates on the highly unpronounceable original name of the character whom we get to know as Ford Prefect:

Example 18

Because Ford never learned to say his original name, his father eventually died of shame, which is still a terminal disease in some parts of the Galaxy.

(Adams 2002: 41, footnote)

The humorousness of the line plays on the conventional, everyday meaning of the phrase 'to die of shame' as a figurative way of saying 'to feel extremely ashamed'. Here, the verb 'to die' is given back its literal sense, suggesting that shame can in fact lead to death. The word 'still' in '[shame] is still a terminal disease' implies that the 'shame' disease used to be a problem in the whole of the Galaxy, indicating perhaps that the origins of the phrase 'to die of shame' were literal. The presentation of death here relies on two different types of humorous distancing. Firstly, by drawing on our knowledge of the conventional meaning of 'to die of shame', the narrator emphasizes the figurative sense of 'to die' as it is used in the phrase, increasing our detachment from the more serious, emotionally charged, literal meaning of it. We are thus temporarily distanced from the negative associations of the general concept of death. This is enhanced by the second type of distancing – the manipulation of the distance between the reader and the particular death described in the narrative world. Even though Ford Prefect is one of the main characters in the novel, the mention of his father's death is rather superficial – it is a passing digression that, being part of a footnote, is physically separated from the main body of the text. The death occurred in the past and, we can assume, in a remote part of the Galaxy, and therefore is an element of a sub-world that is both spatially and temporally distant from the main text world of the novel. The reader is placed in a 'safe', detached position, far removed from the event. This almost physical distance from the situation, combined with the distance from the literal meaning of death itself, means that the amusement triggered by the humorous mention of it is not likely to be affected by the intrinsic negative charge of the dark element. Such a straightforwardly amusing effect of *The Hitchhiker's Guide* is discussed by one of the Goodreads readers:

> It [the novel] is unlikely to affect you on any deep emotional level and you probably won't spend sleepless nights thinking about it.
> But it's a simple, humorous sci-fi adventure.

Adams' writing, the reader suggests, is a 'simple' humorous science-fiction novel, unlikely to trigger serious, negative emotional responses.

The way it distances the reader from the death of a character's relative can be seen as an effect of the author's decision to evoke amusement rather than exploit the potential negative emotional charge of the element in order to achieve a more complex humorous response.

How, then, can a dark element such as the death of a relative be manipulated to result in a more mixed response of amusement and negative emotion? A useful starting point in the search of death-based mood blends is Joseph Heller's war novel *Catch-22*, whose comedy is firmly rooted in the tragedy of war. The comic surface, as remarked by one reviewer, is underlined by inescapable tragedy: 'Sure, it's been funny. But all along the comedy has been an expression of horror' (*The Guardian*, 2011, Chris Cox 'Catch-22: 50 years later'). Comedy as an expression of horror, where the horror retains its emotional impact, must be based on mood blends that result in the combination of amusement and other, negative, emotions. A particularly painful (and amusing) example of this is the following scene from *Catch-22*, in which Yossarian, the protagonist, is asked to lie in a hospital bed and pretend that he is the dying son of a family he had never met. The real son, Giuseppe, is already dead by the time his family arrive to say their final goodbyes to him, and the doctors ask Yossarian to 'fill in' so that the family do not have to leave disappointed:

Example 19 (a)

'It all sounds a bit crazy,' Yossarian reflected. 'What do they want to watch their son die for, anyway?'

'I've never been able to figure that one out,' the doctor admitted, 'but they always do. Well, what do you say? All you've got to do is lie there a few minutes and die a little. Is that asking so much?'

(Heller 1994: 211)

Yossarian finally agrees and, wrapped in bandages and placed in a dimly lit room, he is visited by three members of the family – the mother, the father and the brother – who are led to believe that he is their dying relative. Yossarian initially introduces himself as 'Yossarian' instead of

'Giuseppe', which the family try to play along with, as they take it as a sign of their relative's deteriorating condition. This leads to confusion, as in the end no one knows how to address the 'patient', including the 'patient' himself:

Example 19 (b)

Yossarian remembered suddenly why they were all crying, and he began crying too. A doctor Yossarian had never seen before stepped inside the room and told the visitors courteously that they had to go. The father drew himself up formally to say goodbye.

'Giuseppe,' he began.
'Yossarian,' corrected the son.
'Yossarian,' said the father.
'Giuseppe,' corrected Yossarian.
'Soon you're going to die.'
Yossarian began to cry again. The doctor threw him a dirty look from the rear of the room, and Yossarian made himself stop.

(Heller 1994: 214)

The paradoxical phrase 'die a little' in Example 19 (a) has the potential to both distance the reader from the concept of death in a similar way to 'die of shame' in the Adams extract (Example 18) above. The modifier 'a little' seems incongruous, as it would normally be expected to accompany metaphorical meanings of the word 'die'. Here, the death is supposed to be literal (as far as the soldier's parents are concerned), and so the doctor's use of the phrase 'die a little' highlights the fact that the dying in the following scenes will not be real, as the whole situation is a set-up. The internal incongruity of the phrase, combined with the fake, fabricated nature of the narrative events, help to distance the reader from the negative associations of the original 'death of a relative' element. This distance allows us to see the absurd in Example 19 (b), where everyone's, especially Yossarian's, confusion is humorously exaggerated.

What may not be immediately apparent from these short extracts but is noticeable in the wider context of the narrative is that the absurd humour here is underlined by acute tragedy. This is how one of the Goodreads users describes his/her experience of the novel:

> *Catch-22* reminds me a lot of those comedy/tragedy masks – you know the ones that are supposed to represent like, fine theater or something? Not that I'm comparing *Catch-22* to some great Italian opera. All I'm saying is that the book oscillates cleverly between the absurdly humorous and the grievingly tragic.

The most arresting quality of *Catch-22*, as the reader suggests, is the way it manages to fluctuate smoothly between the seemingly contrasting modes of comedy and tragedy. The tragic does not occur in order to enhance the comic, and neither does the comic simply emphasize the tragic. Rather, the tragedy and the comedy exist in symbiosis, where each is allowed to evoke a powerful emotional effect. Like many of the novel's scenes, the death of a relative passage is therefore constructed to be as humorous as it is disturbing. We are made aware that the final goodbye has been prefabricated and that the patient is only dying 'a little', but our amusement is likely to be affected by the vivid visual and emotional detail of the otherwise heartbreaking scene. The painful detail is hard to disregard, as we are made to adopt Yossarian's point of view, meaning that we are placed in the middle of the action – the patient's bed, in fact. Having been encouraged to view the textual events from up close, we may not achieve a state of complete detachment required for pure amusement, even if the textual events have been manipulated to trigger a humorous response. The key difference between this use of the 'death of a relative' element and the one mentioned in relation to *The Hitchhiker's Guide*, then, is the distance from which the reader is encouraged to view the humorously distorted tragic situation in the narrative world. A mood blend is most likely to occur when the techniques which distance us from the emotional weight of the dark element are accompanied by those devices which simultaneously decrease the distance between us and that element as it appears in the narrative world.

3.4. Conclusion

Writers of comic narratives depend on being able to cue their readers into detached, non-serious, playful cognitive and affective states which facilitate amusement as a preferred response to their texts – the humorous mode and the humorous mood. While the cognitive humorous mode is the knowledge that something is intended to be amusing, the affective humorous mood is the feeling that something is amusing; in comic narratives, they can both be signalled with the use of stabilizing cues that communicate the humorous nature of the text. These cues, as inferred from the openings of a number of comic narratives, include a range of distancing techniques that encourage detachment from textual events, and downgrading devices that help to present those events as laughable. While stabilizing cues help to establish a humorous mode/mood congruent with amusement, many comic novels and short stories will also make use of negatively charged dark elements that trigger effects seemingly unrelated to humour. Although some dark elements can be used specifically for humour creation (as is the case with dark humour), often they act so as to shift the mood from humorous to more solemn, thus allowing for moments of painful emotion. Using dark elements in an otherwise amusing context can also lead to situations where the humorous and the non-humorous blend into one, triggering complex humorous responses based on the simultaneous experience of contrasting emotions. Such emotional blends are made possible through specifically designed configurations of narrative distance and immersion.

4

Engaging with characters

Characterization techniques play a vital role in shaping our emotional experience of reading comic narratives. They allow writers to manipulate representations of people for comic effect, as well as evoke non-humorous emotions associated with engaging with characters more generally. Those characterization strategies used to build laughable characters and manufacture funny interactions act as cues which stabilize amusement as a response to the narrative world. Those which lead us to immerse ourselves in the world by forming attachments to text-based people, on the other hand, can destabilize the humorous response by triggering a range of non-humorous emotional reactions to narrative characters and their affairs.

4.1. Theoretical background

4.1.1. Approaches to emotions evoked by people in narratives

Emotional engagement with people in narratives relies on our ability to create mental models of them based on our interpretation of textual input. In his approach to characterization based on research in social cognition, Culpeper (2000, 2001) suggests that our perceptions of literary/media characters are guided by the same processes as our perceptions of real people. Very often, in order to simplify the complex task of impression formation, we rely on our knowledge of people 'in general' to perceive others not as individuals, but as members of social groups with which we are familiar. This general knowledge of people is said to be stored in networks referred to as *social schemata*. Some of the schemata will carry emotional connotations: *attitude schemata* (van Dijk, e.g. 1989) are the positive or negative evaluations of particular social groups, driven not by personal opinions, but rather by more general aspects of prevailing ideologies.

The idea that some social groups – and therefore some people – are more likeable than others has been explored in psychological approaches to entertainment in order to explain our appreciation for films and television programmes. The concept of *character liking* (e.g. Raney 2004, see also 2006) is based on the idea that our enjoyment of narratives stems from our engagement with characters: watching our favourite characters succeed is thought to be one of the main sources of narrative-induced gratification. Another way of accounting for our pleasure in engaging with fictional characters is through the application of the psychological theory of *mindreading* (Baron-Cohen 1995) to the study of literature. Mindreading is the ability to imagine the thoughts and feelings of others – a skill which can be applied not only in our interactions with real people, but also in response to fictional characters. One of the main pleasures of reading, it has been suggested, lies in testing how well we can infer fictional people's thoughts and feelings (Zunshine 2006). While both character liking and mindreading provide an insight into the ways in which we engage with characters, these notions are only a background to the research on the emotions evoked by people who populate narrative worlds.

In psychological approaches to literature, film and television, our affective responses to characters are often grouped into the three broad categories of *sympathy*, *empathy* and *identification*. Sympathy and empathy are closely related. From a literary linguistic perspective, Stockwell (2009) suggests that the two responses can be explained with the use of the same metaphor, READING IS INVESTMENT, where readers are said to invest in fictional characters in order to gain affective returns (Stockwell 2009: 94, see also Tan 1994, 1995 for emotional returns in films). Apart from the general distinction between empathy as 'feeling with the character' and sympathy as 'feeling for the character', the difference between them can be described in cognitive stylistic terms, which help to relate these two responses to the ways in which real-world readers inhabit narrative worlds. While sympathy involves a reader in the real world simply observing a character in a narrative world, empathy relies on a deeper 'trans-world mapping' between the real-world reader and the narrative character (Stockwell 2009: 93). In her literary approach to empathy, Keen defines it as the 'vicarious, spontaneous sharing of affect' (Keen 2007: 4) which can be triggered by witnessing – whether in person or by reading – someone else's condition. The main narrative techniques used by authors to facilitate empathy, Keen suggests (2006: 216), can be divided into those that manipulate the *narrative situation* (e.g. perspective, mediation between author and reader) and those that increase *character identification* (e.g. naming, traits, quality of speech). Identification, then, is a prerequisite to empathy. It is the feeling of affinity towards the character which enables us to mentally put ourselves in his or her position in order to understand (and share) their feelings, motivations and goals (Oatley 1994, Cohen 2006).

4.1.2. Social aspects of humour

The theories of humour most concerned with representations of other people are those which focus on others as objects of humour – referred to as superiority, disparagement or hostility theories. With their origins linked to Plato and Aristotle (Zillmann 1983, Morreall 1987a, Ferguson and Ford 2008), they are said to have emerged in times when laughter was more often than today seen as an expression of delight at other people's misfortunes, suffering and physical infirmities (Billig 2005: 40). This unfavourable view of humour is also linked to the work of Hobbes, who saw laughter as resulting from a feeling of *Sudden Glory*, induced in people 'either by some sudden act of their own, that pleaseth them; or by the apprehension of some deformed thing in another, by comparison whereof they suddenly applaud themselves' (Hobbes [1651] 1996: 43).

Others' inferiority as a source of amusement was also emphasized by Bergson, who argued that a person's flaws can be seen as humorous as long as they are not presented so as to evoke sympathy for the disparaged subject – laughing at someone requires us to suspend any other emotion we feel for them (Bergson 1913: 139).

The early superiority-based theories of humour emerged in philosophy, and subsequently advanced into such areas as psychoanalysis and experimental social psychology, where disparagement humour began to be studied as one of the various existing types of humour. Freud, for example, distinguished aggressive, cynical or obscene *tendentious jokes* from those which are *non-tendentious* – 'abstract' or 'innocent' ([1905] 1960: 107). The reception of tendentious jokes that disparage particular social groups has since been empirically tested, suggesting that our amusement is likely to result from mocking someone belonging to a social group that we are not part of, or one with which we simply do not identify (Wolff et al. 1934: 341). In the ensuing *disposition theory of humour* (Zillmann and Cantor [1976] 1996), the dichotomy-based notion of associating/disassociating ourselves with particular groups has been replaced by a more fluid continuum of *affective disposition*, where clear-cut group membership is replaced by the scale of our attitudes towards others. Humour appreciation, argue Zillmann and Cantor, is negatively correlated with our liking for the person who is the target of the joke, and positively correlated with our liking for the person who is telling the joke. A disparaging joke, then, is most successful when it is told by our friend and directed at our enemy.

4.2. *Stabilizing cues*: Populating the world with laughable characters

4.2.1. Humorous stereotypes

One particularly effective way of representing narrative characters as objects of humour is through labelling and pigeonholing individuals as members of social groups that are presented as transparent and homogenous. Stereotyping, that is, classifying people as prototypical members of such culturally-constructed social categories, allows us to access stores of knowledge about those categories in a fast, efficient way. While such quick assessment of others is particularly useful in processing short humorous texts such as jokes or gags, it can also allow us to form mental models of humorous characters in more complex narratives. Characterization in comic narratives often relies on writers manipulating easily accessible stereotypes for a humorous effect, for example by exaggerating them, like in the following example from Sue Towsend's *The Secret Diary of Adrian Mole, Aged 13¾*:

Example 20

Sean O'Leary is nineteen today. He has invited me to his birthday party. It is only over the road so I won't have far to go.

I am writing up my diary now just in case I have one too many. People seem to get drunk just stepping over the O'Learys' threshold.

(Townsend 2002: 129)

Although much of the humour here stems from the narrator's interpretation of the situation (Adrian Mole's narration will be discussed further in this chapter), it could also be argued that the extract portrays Adrian's neighbours in a humorous manner. Their nationality is not explicitly stated, but 'O'Leary' is a prototypical Irish name which, in the context of the passage, evokes the stereotype of Irish people as heavy drinkers (e.g. Stivers 2000). Here, this stereotype is comically exaggerated by Adrian's observation about the levels of intoxication of the guests attending the Irish family's party, and especially the ease with which they seem to be reaching those levels. Presumably, everyone at the party is already so inebriated that people appear to be getting drunk 'just stepping over the O'Learys' threshold' as if through osmosis. Although such a hyperbolical, figurative comment could potentially be applied to any group of people, the nationality of the hosts adds to the humour, as it builds on a familiar strand in a long tradition of ethnic jokes that focus on excessive alcohol consumption (for ethnic alcohol jokes, see Davies 1998). The characterization of the O'Leary family in this short passage relies on a humorous distortion of a stereotype, meaning that the O'Learys are not presented as a group of individuals with idiosyncratic personalities, but rather as comic stereotypes accessible to those readers who are able to recognize the manipulation of the stereotype.

4.2.2. Humorous roles

While accessing our general knowledge about the stereotypical traits of different social groups can allow us to comprehend humour aimed at other people, reading extended comic narratives such as novels and short stories also demands that we connect to an additional store of knowledge – that of the universal *dramatic roles* which underlie story plots (Culpeper 2001: 87). The concept of dramatic roles is based on the work of Propp ([1968] 1975), who outlines the basic roles typically assumed by characters in tales – for example, the hero or the villain. Propp's inventory is based on simple folktales, and while it may not necessarily be directly applicable to the analysis of contemporary novels, it nevertheless signals that readers familiar with a culture-specific canon of traditional tales will have grown to expect narratives to revolve around a certain cast of characters.

Those expectations, importantly, are tied to generic conventions, meaning that various genres will employ different configurations of stock characters. A discussion of the stock types specific to the genre of comedy can be found in the work of Frye (1957), who uses the classical theory of drama (*Tractatus Coislinianus* and Aristotle's *Poetics*) to suggest the four main classes of figures which form the basis of comic plots: the self-deprecator (*eiron*), the impostor (*alazon*), the buffoon (*bomolochoi*) and the churl (*agroikos*). These groups contain various stock characters – for example, the class of eirons in classical comedy includes the central 'hero' figure, who tends to be involved in a romantic intrigue, and whose will and actions are opposed by an alazon character, often that of 'the heavy father'. While the clashes between the wilful eirons and the blocking alazons form the basis of the comic plot, characters who fall under the bolomochoi (professional fools, clowns, pages, singers) and the agroikos (killjoys, refusers of festivity) categories function so as to 'polarize the comic mood' (Frye 1957: 172). The appearance of humorous stock types, whether or not they can be neatly classified into a number of clear-cut categories, can be said to 'stabilise' comedy by creating an expectation of humour and triggering a humorous response.

What Frye categorizes as the distinct humorous types of obtrusive impostors, entertaining buffoons and surly churls can perhaps be grouped together under one label – the *misfits*.[1] This broad class is, I believe, more applicable to those characters in contemporary comic narratives who, rather than fitting a single stock role, are constructed as more nuanced blends of various qualities – those who can be described as 'round' rather than 'flat' characters (Forster 1927). Misfits, broadly speaking, are characters whose eccentricity causes them to stand out and – often humorously – disrupt the situations in which they find themselves. The misfit is a volatile character whose eccentricity is emphasized, and whose unpredictable behaviour and disregard for social norms become integral, expected features of his or her character. Misfits' offbeat personalities cause them to stand out and disrupt humorously any stability and equilibrium they may find themselves in. A prototypical example of the misfits category is Barry from Nick Hornby's *High Fidelity*. Barry and Dick are Rob's employees in his London-based record store, Championship Vinyl. While Dick's extreme introversion and social awkwardness mean that he is most comfortable when listening to music on his own (an exaggerated stereotype of the social group of 'music geeks'), Barry seems to thrive in the spotlight and revel in causing disruption. One Goodreads reader describes Barry's comic character as follows:

> Especially Barry, who is described by Rob as a '*snob obscurantist*', makes you laugh uncontrollably with his habit of belittling everything, his sneaky tactics of selling records no one has heard of and his interactions with Dick.

Out of all the characters in the novel, the reader chooses to single out Barry as the one who is 'especially' likely to make you laugh. While the comic value of his interactions with other characters (emphasized by the reader above) will be discussed further, here I explore the characterization techniques which add humour to his habits and qualities. Below is an extract from the scene when Barry first appears in the narrative world of *High Fidelity*, turning up to work late and disturbing Dick and Rob's quiet afternoon. It is narrated by Rob:

Example 21

He comes into the shop humming a Clash riff. Actually, 'humming' is the wrong word: he's making that guitar noise that all little boys make, the one where you stick your lips out, clench your teeth and go 'DA-DA!' Barry is thirty-three years old.

'Awlright boys? Hey, Dick, what's this music, man? It stinks.' He makes a face and holds his nose. 'Phwooar.' […]

Barry puts his hand into his leather jacket pocket, produces a tape, puts it in the machine and jacks up the volume. Within seconds the shop is shaking to the bass line of 'Walking On Sunshine', by Katrina and the Waves. It's February. It's cold. It's wet. Laura has gone. I don't want to hear 'Walking On Sunshine'. Somehow it doesn't fit my mood.

(Hornby 1995: 34–5)

There are a number of discernible techniques here which contribute to Barry's characterization as a misfit. Firstly, he is built through a manipulation of certain stereotypes, mostly those related to the intensity of personal traits and habits, and their suitability to a particular age group. Barry is a 'card' (Harvey 1966) – a 'larger than life' character who is 'an exaggerated prototype of some social category' (Culpeper 2001: 88). Barry, like many comic characters, is built on a manipulated stereotype. Even though it is difficult to pinpoint the single social group which is being distorted here, it can be argued that Barry is a magnified prototype of the category of extroverts. His overblown self-confidence manifests itself in the way he loudly and impolitely occupies the space, his behaviour likened to that of a little boy. In the eyes of

Rob, Barry comes across as a slightly irksome eccentric – the comment 'Barry is thirty-three years old' acts as an antithesis to the description of his strikingly childlike demeanour, emphasizing the oddity of Barry's personality.

The fact that Rob, the protagonist, is prone to getting irritated with Barry is significant, as it highlights Barry's role as one of the impostors in the humorous world of *High Fidelity*. Impostors, as mentioned before, are often the characters who block the hero's actions and desires, interfering and creating obstacles that form the basis of the comic action. By invading Rob's peaceful afternoon (especially on the day after his girlfriend Laura had left him) with his mocking comments and his obnoxious music, Barry creates disruption that, in the following paragraphs, spurs Rob to act. Barry's boorishness, particularly his rude criticism about the music in the shop and subsequent imposition of his own tape, can be linked to the comic function of a churl, who deprives others of joy and enforces his own order. His impoliteness, while off-putting for the other characters, can potentially have an entertaining effect on the reader, thus showcasing his additional role as a convivial, merry-making buffoon. Barry's choice of music, the exceedingly cheerful 'Walking On Sunshine', expresses his tendency, or perhaps desire, to be the life and soul of the party – in this case not appreciated by his co-workers.

One final element of Barry's characterization as a misfit regards the level of attention he is made to attract, both from the other characters and from the reader. His appearance in the shop is impossible to ignore, as he seems to take over the space completely by appealing to various components of our sensory experience. The compelling sensory stimuli he produces range from visual (facial expressions) to auditory (humming, playing music), tactile (making the room shake) and appealing to olfactory (when he fakes smelling an odour). Drawing on elements of our sensory perception when reading narratives (see Sanford and Emmott 2012: 132 for *embodied understanding*), while not directly related to focus and attention, in the example above is magnified so as to make Barry's character stand out from the others in a way typical for the category of misfits. Stylistically, Barry's arresting presence be explained with reference to Stockwell's (2009) notion of *textual attractors*. Attractors are elements in the text which capture the reader's attention, and typically include features like agency, activeness, brightness, fullness, largeness, noisiness and aesthetic distance from the norm (Stockwell 2009: 25). In Barry's case, the most apparent quality is that of noisiness – his distinctive humming and blaring music – but the agency, activeness and fullness in his description are also highlighted by the use of the active voice, action verbs and references to the loudness of his music. Although colours are not explicitly mentioned, it is interesting to note the juxtaposition of 'Sunshine' brought by Barry (in 'Walking On Sunshine') with Rob's 'It's February. It's cold. It's wet.' evocative of a grey winter's day. While each of the attractors can contribute to the characterization of a misfit, the one which seems particularly appropriate is the one that Stockwell terms 'aesthetic distance from the norm', which includes, for example, 'beautiful or ugly referents, dangerous referents, alien objects denoted, dissonance' (2009: 25). A misfit is constructed and presented to stand out from the norm and create disruption. Barry, with his overblown, childlike extroversion, his off-putting gestures and grimaces, and his unpredictable behaviour which disturbs others, illustrates considerable aesthetic distance from the norm.

    A prototypical misfit is a character who attracts attention, fills the comic role of an impostor, a buffoon or a churl (or all of them), and who is built from exaggerated traits. While misfits' disruptive, inappropriate behaviour certainly contributes to advancing the comic plot and to the creation of humour, in some cases it has another social function, that of pushing the limits of what is socially acceptable in a given culture. The role of comedy and ridicule in subverting the social order will be expanded on in the following section, where I discuss some of the destabilizing qualities of character humour. Here, the focus is on constructing misfits as 'the other' – the unadjusted, abnormal, eccentric outsiders, whose lack of conformity with 'our' norms sets them up as targets of laughter. This 'us versus them' dynamic in comedy complies with the superiority theories of humour discussed before, where those who laugh and those who are laughed at are said not to share a common ground. As Gray suggests, 'the comedy of eccentricity', where the eccentric individual is at odds with the world and – to our amusement – loses, functions as a proof of our superiority as well as an act of social exclusion (Gray 2005: 148). This kind of mocking ridicule of what can be considered culturally inappropriate, according to Billig, protects the codes of daily behaviour, ensuring conformity with social order (Billig 2005: 202).

4.2.3. Humorous interactions

Some of the specific codes of behaviour which can be successfully manipulated for comic effect relate to conversational norms. In comic narratives, humorous verbal interactions between characters are often based on communication breakdowns, blunders, vulgarity and other instances where it is possible to detect the incongruity between what would be expected as cooperative (in the Gricean sense, 1975) and that which is surprising, awkward or disruptive. The two key groups of techniques for manufacturing that kind of inappropriate conversational behaviour found in comic narratives are those which (1) produce miscommunication, and those which (2) generate impoliteness in character interactions. Both can be found in the following example from *High Fidelity*, where Rob is trying to understand the full meaning of the word 'yet' after his ex-girlfriend, Laura, who left him for someone else, admits that she has not consummated her new relationship *yet* ('We've slept together but we haven't made love. Not yet.' – Hornby 1995: 87). Jealousy-stricken (but also vaguely hopeful), he attempts to coax the connotations of 'yet' from Barry, trying to predict what Laura is going to do based on her use of the adverb. Rob's indirectness and Barry's qualities of a misfit lead to a rather uncooperative exchange:

Example 22

What does 'yet' mean, after all? 'I haven't seen *Reservoir Dogs* yet.' What does that mean? It means you're going to go, doesn't it?

'Barry, if I were to say to you that I haven't seen *Reservoir Dogs* yet, what would that mean?'

Barry looks at me.

'Just … come on, what would it mean to you? That sentence? "I haven't seen *Reservoir Dogs* yet"?'

'To me, it would mean that you're a liar. Either that or you've gone potty. You saw it twice. Once with Laura, once with me and Dick. We had that conversation about who killed Mr Pink or whatever fucking colour he was.'

'Yeah, yeah, I know. But say I hadn't seen it and I said to you, "I haven't seen *Reservoir Dogs* yet", what would you think?'

'I'd think, you're a sick man. And I'd feel sorry for you.'

(Hornby 1995: 111–12)

While much of the humorous potential of the exchange can largely be attributed to Barry's lack of concern for social conventions, Rob (more specifically, his indirectness) can be held responsible for the amusing miscommunication that occurs. Instead of being open about his motive and asking 'Laura said she hadn't slept with her new boyfriend "yet". Do you think she's going to do it?', he places the word 'yet' in an unrelated context, 'I haven't seen *Reservoir Dogs* yet', and – rather ambiguously – asks 'what would that mean?' Rob's turn is problematic, as it seems to be lacking a referent that specifies what the verb 'mean' refers to. The utterance which he intends to convey – 'what would that mean *about the word "yet"*?' – Barry interprets as 'what would that mean *about me?*' As a result of this ambiguity they begin talking at cross-purposes in a way that may be frustrating to them, but is likely to be amusing to the reader who has access to Rob's thoughts and is able to spot the incongruity between the intended meaning and the inferred meaning. The contrast here is between the different contextual 'lenses' which Rob and Barry are using to interpret the same situation, where Rob's emphasis is on the abstract notion of word meaning, and Barry is focusing on the more down-to-earth aspects of using pop culture references.

While the amused reader recognizes that the miscommunication is likely to be frustrating to the participants, Barry's response is still surprisingly impolite, given the relatively innocuous subject matter. A lack of reply to a direct question ('Barry looks at me.'), name-calling ('liar', 'sick man'), swearing ('fucking') and a general lack of sympathy or interest in what Rob is trying to get across can all be seen as impoliteness strategies that threaten Rob's feelings and identity. Specifically, they can be classified as *positive impoliteness output strategies* associated with attacking someone's positive self-image (Culpeper 1996: 357-358). This positive self-image is referred to as *positive face* (based on Goffman's ([1967] 1972) concept of *face*), and it can be damaged by certain face-threatening acts (FTAs), which, according to Brown and Levinson's (1987) politeness theory, include expressions of disapproval, criticism, ridicule, insults, contradictions, disagreements, challenges and blatant non-cooperation in an activity (1987: 67), many of which can be found in Example 22 above. Aside from complying with the notions from traditional politeness research, Barry's behaviour can be viewed as impolite with reference to more contemporary approaches within pragmatics, such as Bousfield's:

> [...] impoliteness constitutes the issuing of intentionally gratuitous and conflictive verbal face-threatening acts (FTAs) which are purposefully performed unmitigated, in contexts when mitigation is required, and/or, with deliberate *aggression*, that is, with the face threat exacerbated, 'boosted', or maximised in some way to heighten the face damage inflicted.
>
> (Bousfield 2008: 262)

Barry's FTAs certainly seem intentionally gratuitous and deliberately aggressive, as they would have easily been avoided had he chosen to be cooperative. The question remains, however, whether they occurred in one of the 'contexts when mitigation is required'. On the one hand, Rob is Barry's boss and therefore the power dynamics would typically mean that Barry's FTAs should be mitigated to avoid the damage to Rob's face. The social distance between them, however, is likely to be small, as they have known each other for years and frequently socialize together (*power* and *social distance* are variables used by Brown and Levinson 1987 to estimate the seriousness of a face threat). The apparent intimacy between Rob and Barry can in fact lead us to assume that, in the context in which it occurs, the interaction between them could be treated not as impoliteness, but as *banter*. That hypothesis proves incorrect, however, once our knowledge of the narrative world is applied to the definition of banter, as outlined in Leech (1983). According to Leech's *Banter Principle*, banter arises when 'In order to show solidarity with h[earer],' speaker says 'something which is (i) obviously untrue, and (ii) obviously impolite to h', as what speaker 'really means is polite to h and true' (Leech 1983: 144). It would be difficult to argue that Barry says something which is 'obviously untrue' – nothing in his exchange with Rob suggests that he is not being genuine. While he is certainly being 'obviously impolite', there is no reason to believe that he does it to 'show solidarity' with Rob, especially if we take into account what we know about his character. Our knowledge of Barry is, as outlined before, that he is a disruptive misfit who provokes others by disobeying social conventions, including conversational norms associated with mitigating politeness. While the context of the interaction could facilitate banter between a different pair of participants, Barry's personality overshadows contextual constraints and leads him to being intentionally, deliberately aggressive.

Verbal aggression, although potentially hurtful to the hearer, can have an entertaining effect on a distanced observer, such as a reader or a viewer. In his discussion of *entertaining impoliteness*, Culpeper (2011) suggests that contemporary television chat shows, quiz shows, talent shows and other 'docu-soaps' have developed their own, highly entertaining, variants of verbal impoliteness which attract viewers in the way violent sports have done for centuries (2011: 234). He also points out the humorous potential of such linguistic violence, suggesting that that the television genre with the highest levels of verbal aggression is comedy (2011: 234, based on Chory 2010). Some film dialogue, according to Dynel (2013), also relies on this sort of *disaffiliative humour* which showcases the joker's wit for the benefit of the observer, and allows the viewer to feel superior to the target of the joke (the 'pleasure of being superior' is also one of the pleasures of entertaining impoliteness, as outlined by Culpeper 2011: 235). While the link between entertaining impoliteness/disaffiliative humour and superiority over the target of aggression are valid in many cases (as Culpeper and Dynel show), they do not seem to match the *High Fidelity* example analysed here (Example 22). That is because the butt of impoliteness and the object of humour are not the same person. Even though it is Rob who is the target of Barry's insults, the character who is presented as odd and laughable to the reader (and has been since the beginning of the novel) is Barry, the misfit. As distanced observers, we may be amused by the interaction, but we are not likely to be laughing at Rob. That is because Rob is 'one of us' – someone who, unlike the socially maladjusted misfit Barry, has been constructed to trigger identification, sympathy and empathy.

4.3. *Destabilizing cues*: Building emotional engagement with the protagonist

While there are a number of stylistic techniques which can cue the reader to laugh *at* comic characters, writers of comic narratives can also destabilize this amusement by triggering non-humorous emotion, often through manipulating our relationship with the protagonist. In what follows, I show how our attachment to comic heroes can blend the boundary between laughing *at* and laughing *with* characters, resulting in more complex emotional responses to character humour.

4.3.1. The *everyman/everywoman* protagonist

In many of the examples of character humour discussed above, the laughable character (the misfit) is presented to the reader from the point of view of a more 'average' first-person narrator who acts as a backdrop to the other's eccentricity. It is the contrast between the misfit and the more ordinary main character that often leads to humour, as it allows the exaggerated qualities of the misfit to truly shine. Apart from emphasizing the humorous peculiarity of the other, however, the ordinariness of the protagonist has additional functions and a long tradition in narrative comedy. As suggested by Frye (1957), in the low mimetic 'new comedy' of the classical period, which laid foundations for the genre as we know it today, characters were created to be on the level of the audience (e.g. they did not have special powers) so as to inspire identification. In that kind of comedy, suggests Frye, 'the hero himself is seldom a very interesting person: in conformity with low mimetic decorum, he is ordinary in his virtues, but socially attractive' (1957: 44). The comic hero typically belongs to the character category of *eirons*, self-deprecators – a 'self-deprecating or unobtrusively treated character' faced with obstacles that need to be overcome (often related to reuniting with a lover) in order for a happy ending to occur (Frye 1957: 365).

In contemporary comic narratives, that kind of a plot trajectory can be associated with romantic comedies, and therefore it is the subgenre of romantic comedy where prototypical self-deprecator-type protagonists are likely to be found. Hornby's *High Fidelity* is a quintessential rom-com, where the hero (Rob) is separated from his lover (Laura) and complications occur as he faces opposition from a number of blocking characters (including Barry discussed above), but he eventually reunites with his partner in a happy ending. Rob's role in the narrative is summarized by one of the novel's readers on Goodreads:

Rob, the main character, is quite obviously meant to be identified with.

Rob's qualities as a prototypical comic hero come across not only as a result of the contrast with the misfits who stand in his way, but also through constant, direct access to his thoughts, some of which are self-reflections. In the following extract, Rob is introducing himself to the reader in a way which clearly illustrates his characterization as a classic self-deprecator figure:

Example 23

My genius, if I can call it that, is to combine a whole load of averageness into one compact frame. I'd say that there were millions like me, but there aren't, really: lots of blokes have impeccable music taste but don't read, lots of blokes read but are really fat, lots of blokes are sympathetic to feminism but have stupid beards, lots of blokes have a Woody Allen sense of humour but look like Woody Allen. Lots of blokes drink too much, lots of blokes behave stupidly when they drive cars, lots of blokes get into fights, or show off about money, or take drugs. I don't do any of these things, really; if I do OK with women it's not because of the virtues I have, but because of the shadows I don't have.

(Hornby 1995: 22)

The passage can be seen to demonstrate the characterization of Rob as a protagonist who is, in Frye's words, 'ordinary in his virtues, but socially attractive'. Below, I outline the key techniques which add to presenting the hero as an 'attractive everyman'. Aside from appearing in the extract above, these devices contribute to the characterization of Rob throughout the whole novel, and indeed can be found in other comic narratives with an *everyman* or *everywoman* protagonist.

(i)   The comic protagonist as 'one of us'

The first step in creating a comic hero who is ordinary seems to require choosing a particular demographic towards whom the narrative is aimed, as the character's average qualities will only be recognized as average by readers who share a certain sociocultural background. Rob, who emphasizes his ordinariness from the beginning of *High Fidelity*, opens the narrative with a description of his unremarkable teenage years in 1970s suburban England (including 'I lived in Hertfordshire, but I might just as well have lived in any suburb in England', Hornby 1995: 1) – likely to be considered ordinary by those whose stereotypical knowledge of what is 'average' has been shaped by a biography similar to Rob's. Since Hornby's novel came out in 1995 in the United Kingdom, it is not unreasonable to assume that many of its first readers would have spent their teenage years in Britain, some of them in the 1970s. The readers who see Rob as average because they have had similar life trajectories (which they think of as average) can be said to relate to him through what Sanford and Emmott call *autobiographical alignment* (2012: 211), based on sharing some of the qualities of a character. The role of autobiographical alignment in creating a relatable protagonist can also be seen in Example 23 above, where the mention of more specific personal traits can lead some readers to 'align' themselves with Rob if they, too, consider themselves to have a good music taste, interest in books, sympathy towards feminism and a sense of humour. This is how one Goodreads user describes his relationship with Rob:

> Swap out records for video games, and I am Rob. If you're a geek, and a male, and a member of these recent generations of 'slackers' or 'man-children', then you are Rob, too.

According to the concept of autobiographical alignment – and illustrated by the comment above – the reader who finds Rob average and therefore relatable, is a reader who shares Rob's characteristics, from his interests and political views to his age, nationality and life story – ideally, a white, middle-class, left-leaning English man in his thirties whose primary interests are pop culture and romantic relationships. While it is likely that some of the most avid readers of *High Fidelity* (like the reader quoted above) share those characteristics, it would be incorrect to assume that – both in the case of this novel and more generally – common autobiographical details are the only route to identification with the protagonist.

For the readers lacking the common autobiographical ground, the example above provides clues not as to what is 'normal' perhaps, but as to what is *desirable*. By describing himself through a series of oppositions, Rob creates an outline of his own character not through any special features of his own qualities, but through contrast with the negative, unattractive traits he does not have. Not reading books, being really fat, having a stupid beard and looking like Woody Allen are undesirable qualities which, according to Rob, 'lots of blokes' have. 'Lots of blokes', similarly, 'drink too much, lots of blokes behave stupidly when they drive cars, lots of blokes get into fights, or show off about money, or take drugs.' By listing these negative qualities which allegedly many other men possess, Rob not only pictures himself as unique (despite his ordinariness), but also creates the boundaries of a certain social category – 'nice guys' – of which he sets himself as a prototypical member. That category, which excludes traits such as 'gets into fights' but includes ones like 'reads books', is one which is not as unique as Rob makes it out to be. In fact, it is a category which many of the readers of *High Fidelity* are likely to identify with. It is so inclusive, actually, that most people, including women, should be able to relate to enough of the 'nice guys' traits to feel part of the group – especially since the only alternative seems to be the substance-abusing, aggressive social category of 'bad guys'. Aligning our personal traits to fit the qualities of a fictional character can be linked to what Stockwell (2009) calls *accommodation*. Just as in spoken interactions we tend to accommodate our speech to those we are talking to, when reading literature, Stockwell suggests, we can accommodate our personality to engage with literary or fictional minds (2009: 152). Much of *High Fidelity* relies on this kind of bond between the reader and the protagonist, which is established early on in the narrative through references to the hero's 'average' life and personality, and which helps us *accommodate towards* Rob (to use Stockwell's term) in situations where we would otherwise be inclined to move 'away', like when he admits to committing morally dubious acts later in the novel. Accommodating our personality to that of a character is vital for building identification.

The importance of identification between the audience and the humorous protagonist can be linked not only to the literary archetype of the 'everyman' hero in classical comedy, but also to the more contemporary theories of socially-based humour discussed in psychology. As outlined previously, jokes about people are said to rely on a mechanism where 'the jokers' and 'the joked at' belong to distinct social groups, and in order to laugh, the hearer needs to identify with the first and feel separate from the latter. Identifying with the comic protagonist – whether through autobiographical alignment or accommodation of personality – is crucial to humour appreciation in those instances where the hero is the joker who targets other characters humorously. The 'us versus them' dynamic is possible to set up through the use of a juxtaposition of specially constructed social categories, like 'good guys' versus 'bad guys' in the example above. Once we align ourselves with the 'good' group and recognize Rob as a prototypical member, we are more receptive to his humour, especially when it is targeted at other characters.

(ii) Perceived closeness of the comic protagonist

The rather simplistic view of group membership and humorous identification outlined above can be linked to La Fave's (1972) notion of *identification classes*, based on the idea that we are likely to laugh *with* those who belong to social groups that we can identify with, and *at* those who do not. A more sophisticated approach – and more relevant to the present discussion – is that of humour appreciation being dependent on a *scale of affective disposition* towards people, where amusement is said to 'be maximal when our friends humiliate our enemies, and minimal when our enemies manage to get the upper hand over our friends' (Zillmann and Cantor 1996 [1972]: 100-1). Here, the idea of identification gives way to that of affective disposition or, simply put, liking. As I will argue, an 'ordinary, but socially attractive' (in Frye's 1957 words) every(wo)man protagonist is not only constructed as a member of an inclusive social category that encourages alignment and accommodation, but also is presented as likeable so as to facilitate those processes.

The techniques associated with creating a likeable comic hero(ine) especially relevant here are those which help to reduce the perceived distance between the character and the reader so as to create a sense of intimacy and communion (Booth's 1961 notion of a *secret communion* between the reader and the author behind the character's back can complicate this relationship, and it will be discussed further). One of the most effective and simple devices for building closeness with a humorous protagonist is the use of first-person narration – in fact, of the twelve texts analysed in this study, eight are narrated by their main characters. The role of first-person perspective in manipulating distance between the reader and the narrative world is discussed by Dancygier (2011), who argues that narrative viewpoint is determined by configurations of three types of spaces: the story-viewpoint space (SV), where the narrator is located; the main narrative (MN) space of the primary plot; and an Ego-viewpoint established when a character in MN is selected as the narrator (2011: 63). She points out that third person narration 'is a device setting up a deictic centre of the narrating subjectivity outside of the main narrative space' which consequently 'distances the main narrative space from the SV-space' (2011: 68) The use of past tense, she suggests, has a similar effect. Other distancing tools mentioned by her include markers of epistemic distance (words such as 'presumably' or 'perhaps'), passive voice and formal vocabulary (2011: 72). None of those, notably, can be found in Example 23, which relies on first-person narration, present tense, active voice and informal diction (e.g. 'blokes', 'I do OK'). The only marker of epistemic modality is the word 'really', which softens the impact of Rob's rather bold statements and perhaps makes him appear less arrogant. These stylistic techniques reduce the distance between Rob and the narrative world, and also between him and the reader, helping to present Rob as a protagonist who is not only relatable, but also possible to connect with. This perceived closeness to the main character is stressed by one of the Goodreads readers of *High Fidelity*:

> Rob is my soul mate, you see. He and I are the same fucked up, insecure, too-much-in-our-own-head-for-our-own-good person. I think he would get me. Really Get me.

The reader's emphasis on Rob being their 'soul mate' and someone who would really 'get' them can be seen as a general effect of those characterization techniques in *High Fidelity* which, as outlined above, allow readers to emotionally connect with the protagonist. The idea of forming emotional connections with people from books, films or television shows has been referred to as the *parasocial interaction* (*PSI*) phenomenon, its primary focus being relationships between audiences and media figures, from celebrities to fictional characters (see Giles 2002 for a review). The term was first coined by Horton and Wohl (1956), who examined the likeability of television personalities (such as chat show hosts) and the *illusion of intimacy* created between them and the viewers. Horton and Wohl outlined a number of strategies used for achieving this illusion in TV audiences, stressing the shows' underlying aim to blur the line between the 'persona' (and his/her show in the studio) and the viewers at home. While the techniques mentioned (e.g. using friendly gestures, addressing other cast members by first names, mingling with the studio audience) are not directly translatable to written narratives and their addressees, it is not difficult to draw an analogy between them and the distance-reducing narrative tools mentioned before.

Aside from reducing distance, a feature of PSI that is particularly relevant to the idea of forming communion with comic protagonists is the tendency of audiences to form *attachments* to fictional figures. Attachment theory (Bowlby, e.g. [1969] 1997) has been applied to explain how viewers' imaginary relationships with media characters are affected by their attachment styles and the ensuing preconceptions about intimacy and loss (e.g. Cohen 2004, Greenwood 2008). Green, Brock and Kaufman (2004) link attachment to immersion in narrative worlds, suggesting that as we become engaged in a narrative world, we may develop a sense of connection with characters encountered repeatedly over time (2004: 319). While in the context of narrative comedy this is especially true of long-running television sitcoms, the idea can also be applied to humorous novels with strong central figures and collections of short stories with a common protagonist.

(iii) The comic protagonist as a self-deprecator

Another characterization strategy used to construct a relatable, likeable every(wo)man comic protagonist is humorous self-deprecation. Self-deprecating humour is that in which the role of the object of laughter – usually reserved for disliked or unaffiliated individuals – is filled by the jokers themselves. This kind of joking is said to have a range of effects, from placing the self-disparager in a positive light by demonstrating his or her modesty, to putting the listeners at ease by ingratiating oneself to them (Zillmann and Stocking 1976, Long and Graesser 1988). The link between the use of self-disparaging humorous remarks and perceived personal attractiveness has been studied in social psychology, with a number of studies suggesting that self-deprecating humour increases desirability if the target is otherwise physically attractive or has a high social status (Lundy, Tan and Cunningham 1998, Greengross and Miller 2008).

For a comic protagonist who is presented as high-status due to his or her central role in the plot and whose attractiveness is enhanced by distance-reducing devices, self-deprecation can be both a source of humour and a means of establishing an equal footing with the reader. *High Fidelity*'s Rob, for example, uses mildly self-disparaging elements to balance his disparagement of other people. He may mock people who 'are really fat' or 'have stupid beards', but he puts himself down while he does it by emphasizing his own averageness and lack of special virtues. That way, the reader can both feel superior towards 'lots of blokes' and their unattractive qualities listed by Rob and towards Rob himself. By showing his humility and allowing us that feeling of superiority, the narrator puts us at ease and reinforces his position as an affable joker, thus giving us permission to laugh at social groups that we would not otherwise be comfortable laughing at. He boosts his own attractiveness while simultaneously generating disparagement-based humour that adds to the humorous quality of the narrative world.

4.3.2. The 'misfit' protagonist

The self-deprecation that is characteristic of the every(wo)man comic protagonist stands in opposition to one particular trait found in the contrasting character category of misfits: narcissism. Narcissistic tendencies of the stock type may have already become apparent in the discussion of *High Fidelity*'s Barry, whose overblown extroversion and disregard for politeness can be seen as symptomatic of an excessive self-centredness and an inflated sense of self-importance. Some comic narratives will rely on clashes between relatable, self-deprecating protagonists and eccentric, narcissistic antagonists to create character humour. Many, however, will blend the two contrasting features to create complex comic protagonists whose relationships with readers are more complicated.

In *High Fidelity*, the prototypical everyman Rob uses self-deprecation to counterweigh his narcissistic remarks about his 'genius' and superiority over 'other blokes' (Example 23). As a quintessential everyman, Rob needs to remain unexceptional and unassuming in order to sustain the reader's identification and positive affect towards him. Although he disparages other men's personal traits for a comic effect, the underlying message of his self-characterization is that he lacks any distinctive qualities of his own. He is, in fact, the epitome of ordinariness, whose main achievement is 'to combine a whole load of averageness into one compact frame'. His boastful remarks, while largely superficial, help to prime a positive reaction to this otherwise unflattering confession of own mediocrity. Their superficiality, once recognized by the reader, helps to showcase him as an attractive character who is not afraid to set himself up as an object of laughter. The ability to put oneself down jokingly is a desirable quality for a protagonist who is otherwise presented as important and appealing. It can be argued, therefore, that Rob's mock narcissism is in fact a self-deprecating strategy that enhances his quality as an ordinary, yet attractive everyman protagonist.

While for many comic heroes and heroines mock narcissism is a means of emphasizing ordinariness and establishing an equal footing with the reader, the levels of awareness with which they use it can be manipulated by the author. Hornby's protagonist seems self-conscious in how he comes across, and we have little trouble reading the intention behind his seemingly boastful comments. That is because he is a *reliable narrator* (Booth 1961: 159), who 'acts in accordance with the norms of the work (which is to say, the implied author's norms)', thus earning the reader's trust. His use of mock narcissism is conscious and premeditated, leaving little doubt as to what the intended meaning is. An *unreliable narrator* (also Booth 1961), on the other hand, presents a different challenge. The following example from *The Secret Diary of Adrian Mole* shows the comic protagonist Adrian as an unambiguously unreliable narrator, whose narcissism cannot be linked to self-deprecation as directly as Rob's:

Example 24

SUNDAY JANUARY 11th
First after Epiphany

Now I *know* I am an intellectual. I saw Malcolm Muggeridge on the television last night, and I understood nearly every word. It all adds up. A bad home, poor diet, not liking punk. I think I will join the library and see what happens.

It is a pity there aren't any more intellectuals living round here. Mr Lucas wears corduroy trousers, but he's an insurance man. Just my luck.

The first what after Epiphany?

(Townsend 2002: 10)

Like Rob, Adrian is a first-person narrator, whose use of present tense, active voice, informal vocabulary and few markers of epistemic modality should in principle reduce the story-narrator distance, as it helps to set the story-viewpoint space within the main narrative space (to use Dancygier's 2011 terminology). Despite being immersed in his narrative world to the extent that he should be a reliable guide, however, Adrian lacks the credibility we would expect from a character to whom we form an attachment. An unreliable narrator, according to Booth, is one who is 'mistaken' or 'believes himself to have qualities which the author denies him' (1961: 159). Adrian's idea of what it takes to be an intellectual (e.g. not liking punk, wearing corduroy trousers) is likely to lead us to think that he is mistaken, and that his assessment of himself as one is wrong. Our judgement is based partly on our own preconceptions of what it means to be an intellectual (which may include 'not labelling people based on their superficial traits'), and partly on the author's rather explicit manipulation of the situation. Adrian's diary entry falls on a Sunday marked as 'First after Epiphany'. As an 'intellectual', he could be expected to know the meaning of that phrase (or at least discover a way of finding out). Instead, he openly reveals his ignorance, closing his entry with 'The first what after Epiphany?', conclusively undermining any claims about his developed intellect that he may have made. Goodreads users, in fact, often discuss those intellect-related aspects of Adrian's characterization, referring to him Adrian as a 'self-styled', 'self-proclaimed' or 'self-classified' intellectual, and emphasizing his lack of self-awareness and tendency towards narcissism:

> Poor old Adrian: so innocent and pompous and self-deluded, all at the same time. [...] Great social document, with some enduring humour – a lot of it in the gap between what Adrian thinks/understands and what the reader understands.

While 'poor old Adrian' remains a relatable and likeable protagonist, his innocent, unformed understanding of the world leads to his lack of reliability as a narrator. This unreliability can lead us to relax the communion we have with him, and instead form a *secret communion* (Booth 1961) with the writer behind the narrator's back. Booth describes the process as:

> [...] though the narrator may have some redeeming qualities of mind and heart, we travel with the silent author, observing as from a rear seat the humorous or disgraceful or ridiculous or vicious driving behaviour of the narrator seated in front. The author may wink and nudge, but he may not speak. The reader may sympathize or deplore, but he never accepts the narrator as a reliable guide.
>
> (Booth 1961: 300)

Adrian can still inspire sympathy and other emotions, but his unreliability widens the distance between him and the reader. This increased emotional distance means that he is more likely to become the object of laughter. Our secret communion with the author allows us to form a reader-writer joking in-group that occasionally targets the protagonist. Adrian's narcissistic remarks about his exceptional intellect are far from being self-deprecating (as was the case with Rob) – rather, they signal his egotistical tendencies, adding to his characterization as an *everyman protagonist with misfit qualities*. Despite being an otherwise likeable and relatable comic hero, his features of a narcissistic misfit allow the author to poke fun at him for our amusement – a humour-creation strategy made possible by the use of unreliable narration.

The protagonist's narcissism can be mild, feigned and used to put oneself down jokingly so as to decrease the reader-character distance; or it can be robust, genuine and imbue the character with amusing misfit tendencies, thus increasing the distance between them and the reader. An interesting mix of the two can be found in the works of David Sedaris, whose autobiographical short stories that centre around him as the comic hero involve complex blends of self-deprecation and narcissism. This complexity can be illustrated by the two, very different, Goodreads reviews of Sedaris' collection *Me Talk Pretty One Day* quoted below, which indicate a range of responses elicited by Sedaris' first-person narration:

> The main character of the book, however, is what ruined it for me. [...] So much of the narration in the book had a tone of arrogance when I could see no reason to be.
>
> One key to humor writing can be self-deprecation, and Sedaris uses it to elicit guffaws at times from his audience.

There seems to be a lack of consensus as to whether the protagonist-narrator is a genuinely arrogant and narcissistic misfit or whether the opposite is true, and his humour is largely self-deprecating, as would be the case for an everyman protagonist. In the following example from the short story 'Smart Guy', Sedaris uses highly pronounced narcissism to express highly pronounced self-deprecation in a way which complicates his status as an *everyman/misfit* protagonist:

Example 25

As a child I'd always harboured a sneaking suspicion that I might be a genius. The theory was completely my own, corroborated by no one, but so what? Being misunderstood was all part of the package. [...] I practiced thoughtfully removing my glasses and imagined myself appearing on one of those Sunday-morning television shows, where I'd take my seat beside other learned men and voice my dark and radical theories on the human condition.

'People are insecure,' I'd say. 'They wear masks and play games.'

My ideas would be like demons rushing from a hellish cave, and my fellow intellectuals, startled by the truth and enormity of my observations, would try to bottle them up before they spread.

(Sedaris 2002: 241-242)

So far, I have suggested that the levels of reader-character distance mean that an every(wo)man is generally a relatable character that we laugh *with*, and a misfit is an eccentric character that we laugh *at*. In stories where main characters are also first-person narrators, this tendency is facilitated by the use of reliable versus unreliable narration, where unreliable narrators are more prone to becoming the targets of the authors' humour. In the case of David Sedaris, the situation is more complicated, in that even though the reader is explicitly led to laugh *at* the main character, it is difficult to classify the first-person narration as unreliable, since the author and the narrator are the same person. Sedaris' narcissism is, then, much more of the feigned, self-deprecating quality observed in the everyman protagonist, Rob. Unlike Rob's narcissism, however, Sedaris' self-reported arrogance is presented as considerably more severe – not entirely typical of an 'average, but socially attractive' relatable comic hero. Despite the underlying everyman-type self-deprecation, the distancing techniques in the description mean that Sedaris comes across as a misfit. Even though he talks about himself, he distances his adult viewpoint from the childhood-based narrative space by using the past tense to refer to imagined scenarios that never actually took place. The spatio-temporal distance between the adult, real-life narrator and the past, imagined version of the narrator can give an impression that the adult 'everyman' David Sedaris is mocking the misfit qualities of his younger self, but that is only partly true. Below is the contemporary Sedaris' comment (also from 'Smart Guy') on the outcome of his Mensa eligibility test, which finally allowed him to find out his IQ score:

Example 26

It turns out that I'm really stupid, practically an idiot. There are cats that weigh more than my IQ score. Were my number translated into dollars, it would buy you about three buckets of fried chicken. The fact that this surprises me only bespeaks the depths of my ignorance.

(Sedaris 2002: 246)

There is very little distancing being used in the first two sentences of the passage (present tense, informal diction), leaving little doubt that the narrator is actually disparaging himself. The subjunctive mood ('Were my number translated…') and the unusually formal diction ('bespeaks the depths') used in the latter part seem to create the distance necessary for the reader to understand that the protagonist is not taking himself seriously and that it is acceptable to laugh – especially that the formal and informal elements of the passage can be said to create a humorous incongruity. The question is – does he want us to laugh *at* him or *with* him?

David Sedaris seems to combine the qualities of a likeable, self-deprecating, relatable everyman protagonist who can laugh at himself with that of a socially maladjusted, arrogant, larger-than-life misfit. Sedaris presents himself as a self-deprecating misfit, and we are encouraged to laugh both with and at him. In an article entitled 'What You Read is What He Is, Sort Of', Sarah Lyall describes the writer's blending of the ordinary and the unusual:

But even the most mundane experience is described through the skewed prism of his unusual sensibility. This makes it far more amusing than if it had happened to a regular person with prosaic powers of description or a lesser ability to find the absurd in the ordinary.

(*The New York Times*, 8 June 2008)

Sedaris is a self-deprecating misfit, and we are encouraged to laugh both with and at him. He may see the world through 'the skewed prism of his unusual sensibility' that can appear odd, eccentric and laughable, but he is 'one of us' in that he shares the mundane, ordinary reality that we can identify with. His less than prototypical qualities single him out as special (or perhaps odd), but the affinity we may have built up for him leads us to accommodate our own personalities to move 'towards' him (in the way suggested by Stockwell 2009, as discussed above). This is how one Goodreads user describes their experience of reading Sedaris' prose:

> I came into this book expecting the voice of a pretentious, self-indulgent white male, and I finished this book smirking along with this funny, pretentious, and self-indulgent white male.

David Sedaris may be a narcissistic eccentric, but by showing off his amusing, awkward qualities he draws our attention to similar qualities of our own, be it unfounded self-admiration or an embarrassingly low IQ. He is a relatable misfit who shows us the misfit part of ourselves – by allowing us to laugh at him, he allows us to laugh at ourselves.

4.3.3. Protagonists in disrupted interaction

One particularly productive source of character humour is witnessing comic protagonists trying to negotiate social situations – and failing humorously. Some of the most amusing scenes in narrative comedy involve the main characters being socially disruptive; doing or saying things that are inappropriate in a particular situation. Not all those scenes, however, are equally funny to everyone, as some readers may find that their amusement is overshadowed by an unpleasant feeling of embarrassment for the character who is behaving inappropriately.

As I show below, our emotional reactions that arise in response to unsuccessful social interactions are shaped, in part, by our relationship with the characters involved in them.

I have suggested that a comic protagonist can be constructed from a combination of ordinary, relatable 'every(wo)man' qualities with eccentric, laughable 'misfit' qualities, and that the ratio of one to the other affects the reader's relationship with him or her. Based on the disposition theory of humour (and of narratives generally, see Raney 2004), the more perceived similarity and the lesser emotional distance between the character and the reader (as in the case of every(wo)man-type protagonist), the less inclined we should be to laugh at them and enjoy their misfortunes. The correlation of identification with a character with hopes for positive outcomes for them can be explained by referring to the concept of empathy, which, as suggested by Davis (1994), is thought to be most powerful when it is a reaction to observing a target similar to us being entangled in a severely adverse situation. Since a high proportion of character humour involves characters – including protagonists – getting in trouble and experiencing misfortunes (as it will be outlined in the following chapter), here I explore the potential emotional reactions that arise when we witness our favourite comic heroes and heroines fail humorously. The focus will be on comic protagonists being socially disruptive – specifically, saying things that can be seen as inappropriate in a particular social situation. It will be suggested that while straightforward amusement is likely to be triggered when observing a misfit protagonist behaving inappropriately in a relatively low-risk situation, it can be destabilized by other emotions (like embarrassment) when our liking for, identification with or reduced distance towards the character and their world leads us to experience empathy, especially in serious, high-risk social situations. While the affinity with the character and the seriousness of the situation will be emphasized as important variables that affect readers' response to protagonists' disruptive behaviour, other, complicating factors will also be taken into account.

(i) Comedy which grants us protection from embarrassment

Protagonists who possess conspicuous misfit qualities are, in many ways, invulnerable to the negative emotional impact associated with disrupted social interaction. Their eccentricity, often accompanied by a disregard for social conventions, acts as a protective layer both for the characters and the readers who witness their behaviour. That is especially true for those protagonists who purposefully set themselves up as amusing misfits, making it their aim to disrupt social situations to entertain others. In his autobiographical account of the Second World War, Spike Milligan proudly characterizes himself as one such misfit:

Example 27

I was the clown of the Battery – I would give a demonstration of how to rifle drill in Braille, how to sleep standing up on guard, how to teach a battledress to beg, how to march standing still.
    Roll call one morning.
    'Neat?'
    'Sah!'
    'Edgington?'
    'Sah!'
    'Milligan ... MILLIGAN? ... GUNNER MILLIGAN?'
    'Sah!'
    'Why didn't you answer the first time?'
    'I thought I'd bring a little tension into your life, Sarge.'

(Milligan 1971: 98)

Milligan recounts deliberately disrupting a morning roll call for others' amusement in what could be expected to be a relatively high-risk social imposition – taking into account the importance of obeying orders and respecting the hierarchy in the army context. Additionally, the narrator is presenting the events in the first person, minimizing the distance between himself and the story and complementing our awareness of the non-fictionality of the narrative. Both the seriousness of the situation and our relationship with the protagonist, however, are mitigated by his own self-characterization as a 'clown'. By setting himself up as someone whose primary concern is to amuse and entertain, Milligan manipulates what is expected from him by other people (fellow characters as well as readers). A clown is a prototypical misfit, and so the social risks he takes do not bother us as much as they would if he were 'one of us'. Even if he gets hurt, his shield of eccentricity protects him (and us) from real damage.

Apart from having potential practical repercussions, the damage associated with being socially disruptive is largely emotional – it is that of experiencing *embarrassment*. Infringing on established norms of interaction, as suggested by Billig (2005: 202), is as embarrassing for the agent as it is comic for the onlookers, making the fear of ridicule a key tool in the maintenance of social conventions. Psychological research views embarrassment, together with shame, pride or guilt, as a self-conscious emotion experienced as a result of evaluating our behaviour according to certain socio-culturally established standards, rules and goals (SRGs) – 'Success or failure vis-à-vis our SRGs is likely to produce a signal to the self that results in self-reflection' and a global evaluation of the self (Lewis 2008: 745). The negative, unpleasant emotion of embarrassment is based on that kind of unfavourable assessment of one's actions (like shame, only less intense), or it can result from unwelcome exposure (e.g. being looked at, being complimented) (Lewis 2008: 750-1). In Example 27 above, Spike Milligan comes across as immune to embarrassment. Far from shying away from exposure, he revels in being the centre of attention like a typical misfit. The SRGs that potentially stop other soldiers from misbehaving seem to have a different meaning to him – rather than evaluating his actions as inappropriate and feeling embarrassment (or shame or guilt), he appears *proud* of himself, as if his self-reflection had been positive instead of negative. Milligan's self-imposed role as a clown allows him to step outside the sociocultural norms and conventions and create his own set of SRGs, thus fulfilling an important social function of comedy, which, as Stewart Lee suggests, is 'to manufacture inappropriate behaviour' (Lee 2010: 241). In a passage on the Pueblo clowns of South America (but which can be applied to other self-made clowns), Lee points out that 'By reversing the norms and breaking the taboos, the clowns show us what we have to lose, and what we might also stand to gain, if we step outside the restrictions of social convention and polite everyday discourse' (Lee 2010: 241). Professional clowns like Spike Milligan can allow us to see that while simultaneously shielding us from the embarrassment we would otherwise risk.

Being protected from the embarrassment associated with humorously disrupted interactions is crucial to the experience of pure, unadulterated amusement. 'Embarrassment, because it erodes the boundary between audience and butt, is a risky option in comedy and is generally kept in check by precise narrative boundaries', suggests Gray in her discussion of the British sitcom (2005: 151). Emphasizing the misfit qualities of the protagonist may be one of the tools for keeping embarrassment 'in check', allowing us to join him or her in a safe private space where embarrassment cannot reach us (Gray 2005: 161). By creating their own private space that is separate from the rest of the narrative world, the misfit protagonists remain unaffected by the emotional consequences of their actions. The 'clown' status grants the comic hero such distance from the world and the standards, rules and goals that regulate the behaviour of its inhabitants. It is especially useful in those narrative worlds which are expected to operate according to rules very similar to the real world of the reader, particularly non-fictional narratives like Milligan's Second World War memoir. Because the world he describes is one that we can be familiar with (if not through experience, through other accounts), Milligan needs to emphasize his special status of a misfit-joker and the ensuing humorous 'private space' that allows him to subvert conventions without risking damage. Through the lens of his eccentric, clownish point of view, the otherwise realistic world of the Second World War in Britain becomes a humorous one, where the levels of absurd behaviour and a suspension of social conventions render the self-reflective emotion of embarrassment redundant.

It is, in fact, not unlike the twisted, fictional, wartime world of Joseph Heller's *Catch-22*, where the overblown misfit qualities of the army commanders lead them to impose their own set of SRGs on the whole regiment in a way that can be seen in the following quote from the novel's Colonel Korn:

Example 28
'You know, that might be the answer – to act boastfully about something we ought to be ashamed of. That's a trick that never seems to fail.'
(Heller 1994: 160)

In a world ruled by misfits who place narcissism over self-deprecation and who can effectively manipulate sociocultural standards of behaviour, the emotion of pride can be caused to replace that of shame – the 'trick' is to project boastfulness onto typically shameful behaviours. The narrative world of *Catch-22* thus seemingly keeps negative self-reflective emotions in check by running on its own set of rules, where eccentricity, arrogance and delusion are desirable. The protagonist, Yossarian, is therefore not embarrassed to lie to doctors about 'seeing everything twice' in order to prolong his stay in the hospital or to have conversations while sitting in the tree naked. His lunacy is mild and it is nothing compared to the insanity of the world he belongs to – in fact, he is the only character who seems acutely aware of the absurd of what is going on around him. In the context that he is in, his socially inappropriate behaviour loses its inappropriateness. Rather than being embarrassed for him, the reader is encouraged to compare his rather harmless disruptive actions to those of his superiors, whose madness affects the lives and wellbeing of others. While Joseph Heller may protect us from embarrassment by not allowing his protagonist to feel that emotion, his narrative has very strong dark undertones of the collective shame that *should* be experienced by those in charge of the military operations. Those readers who vicariously experience that shame (conspicuous by its absence) while simultaneously being amused by the inappropriate behaviour of the novel's misfit characters can fully appreciate the complex humorous responses cued by the author.

(ii) Cringe humour
While some writers will protect their readers from painful emotion, others will incorporate it into the narrative in order to trigger a complex

response where embarrassment and amusement are combined in what can be referred to as *cringe humour* (see e.g. Marszalek 2019, or *cringe comedy* in Woodward 2010, Wright 2011). The emotional experience of that type of humour is succinctly described by one reader of Haddon's *A Spot of Bother* (a comic novel which, as I suggest below, is rich in cringe) as:

> there's a tiny bit of an inward cringe even as you chuckle

The complex humorous response associated with cringe humour in narratives often relies on writers constructing unsuccessful social interactions, where readers' amusement at someone's blunder is evoked alongside the awkwardness they feel once they imagine what it must be like to be in the disrupted situation. As Wright points out in his discussion of Larry David's sitcom *Curb Your Enthusiasm* (HBO, 2000-present), 'cringe humor relies not on the execution of a gag, but instead on the "dead air" that accompanies an unsuccessful social encounter' (Wright 2011: 662). David's *Curb Your Enthusiasm*, together with Ricky Gervais and Stephen Merchant's *The Office* (BBC, 2001-2003), are two recent, highly prototypical cringe comedy texts that centre around the lives of eccentric, self-involved misfit protagonists whose unconventional approach to social norms leads them to cause (often severe) disruption. Rather than trying to conform to what is socially acceptable to avoid ridicule and embarrassment, those characters will say or do the most inappropriate thing in order to show us where the boundaries lie and what happens when we step outside them. The difference between cringe comedy protagonists and the other types of misfits discussed above is that while jokers like Milligan or Yossarian protect us from embarrassment in one way or the other, cringe comedy heroes do not (see Gray 2005 for a discussion of this in *The Office*).

The two discerning features of cringe comedy, suggests Woodward, basing on both David's and Gervais/Merchant's work, are that (1) it shows us the ludicrous, but suggests that real damage has been caused and that (2) it creates an uncomfortable balance in us between feelings of superiority and inferiority (2010: 4), meaning that it causes us to laugh at the misbehaving character while simultaneously leading us to a painful self-reflection. 'The essential poetics of cringe comedy', writes Woodward, is 'this undecidable tension between feeling above the absurd character and his situation and recognizing ourselves in them' (2010: 10). Aside from the uncomfortable feeling of identification triggered by our familiarity with the misfit qualities of the protagonists, much of the cringe in cringe comedy comes from the relative seriousness of the situations that the characters find themselves in. What Woodward refers to as 'real damage caused' in the television context refers to the use of documentary elements that give an impression of realness and authenticity (2010: 4) – TV cringe comedy is often based on setting eccentric misfit protagonists up for ridicule by leading them to disrupt social situations, while emphasizing the authenticity of the narrative world by adopting a documentary or improvised style. In written narratives, the 'real damage' associated with cringe humour is likely to be achieved by different means, since even explicit non-fictionality of the text cannot automatically be expected to expose the reader to embarrassment at the protagonist's misconduct, as illustrated by Spike Milligan's memoir.

The narrative strategy which I will discuss here in relation to the creation of cringe humour in written narratives is that of cueing *empathy* for the comic protagonist. Feeling the character's awkwardness, I believe, requires us to be able to put ourselves in their position and imagine what it would be like from their perspective – a mechanism referred to as *role taking*, considered to be a highly advanced cognitive process which enables empathy (Davis 1994, Zillmann 1991). Of the general antecedents to empathy outlined by Davis (1994), those which can be applied in a narrative context to explain readers' empathetic reactions towards characters are the *strength of the situation* and the *degree of similarity* between the observer and target (Davis 1994: 15). In her literary approach to narrative empathy, Keen distinguishes *narrative situation* and *character identification* as the two main groups of empathetic narrative techniques, which can be seen to correspond with the components of Davis' psychological model. With regard to television cringe comedy which centres on highly eccentric, socially maladjusted misfit protagonists, it can be argued that the production teams of those shows use documentary elements to create an illusion of realness so as to emphasize the seriousness of the disrupted social situation and evoke empathetic responses from viewers. In written narratives, which are perhaps less arresting to the senses than multimodal texts and thus allow receivers to distance themselves from the events depicted more easily, it may be more effective to manipulate the qualities of the target of empathy, increasing the perceived similarity between the reader and the character. The more similarity between them, the stronger the empathetic response will be. Additionally, the target should also be perceived as morally sound, since malevolent characters may not trigger empathetic responses as well as benevolent or neutral ones can (Zillmann and Cantor 1977, Zillmann 2006). On the whole, then, a comic protagonist who is most likely to cue role taking (and cringe) in the reader is one who is perceived as similar and likeable – in short, a protagonist with pronounced 'every(wo)man' qualities.

Due to the role of character identification and the strength of the situation in triggering the role-taking process which enables the cringe in cringe comedy, the clearest examples of that type of humour in written narratives can be found in situations where a likeable, relatable every(wo)man protagonist is put in a particularly high-risk social position. It is not surprising, therefore, that two of the novels with highly ordinary heroes discussed here, *Lucky Jim* and *A Spot of Bother*, culminate in scenes where the protagonists are compelled to give important speeches in front of large audiences. In fact, public speaking – particularly when it goes wrong – seems to be an effective comic trope generally. In 'The Learning Curve', David Sedaris is drawing on his humiliating experiences of it in his account of teaching creative writing (analysed further in the next chapter); one of the climactic scenes of *Right Ho, Jeeves* focuses on the character Gussie Fink-Nottle's intoxicated prize-giving in front of the whole of Market Snodsbury Grammar School; and while Bridget Jones does not do any public speaking in the novel itself, there are two separate instances of her cringeworthy attempts at it in the film version of the narrative (2001, dir. Sharon Maguire). In each of these texts, the characters who are required to speak in front of an audience behave inappropriately – they are either unprepared and lost for words ('The Learning Curve', *Bridget Jones' Diary*) or they are so intoxicated that they are incomprehensible or say unsuitable, offensive things (*Right Ho, Jeeves, Lucky Jim, A Spot of Bother*). In the following extract from *A Spot of Bother*, George pauses his speech at his daughter's wedding reception to reflect to himself on whether mixing sedatives with alcohol prior to speaking, together with mentioning his recent health scare, had been appropriate:

Example 29

George had lost the thread somewhat.

The dessert wine had not sharpened his mind. He had been a good deal more emotional than he had intended. He had mentioned the cancer, which was not festive. Was it possible that he had made a fool of himself?

(Haddon 2007: 474)

George, whose clumsy, improvised wedding speech focuses mostly on the inevitability of death, closes his public appearance by physically attacking one of the guests. In a way typical for cringe comedy, which relies on what Wright (2011) calls the 'dead air' that surrounds awkward social situations, the reader is being kept aware of the stunned silence that accompanies both George's speech and the succeeding assault. Haddon emphasizes the absence of sound by interjecting George's viewpoint with sentence-long paragraphs of omniscient narration that alert the reader to the wedding guests' silence, like 'In a nearby garden Eileen and Ronnie's dog barked.' (2007: 473) or 'It was very, very quiet in the marquee.' (2007: 477). George's point of view in the extended wedding speech scene is also juxtaposed with the viewpoints of his family members, who speechlessly observe his humiliation, trying to assess the damage. Mostly, however, like in the example above, the scene is shown from George's angle with the use of *free indirect thought* (FIT). FIT is a technique of thought presentation which blends the thoughts of the character with those of the narrator/author, therefore making it impossible to determine – by using linguistic criteria alone – whose thoughts we are reading (Leech and Short 2007: 271). In terms of cringe humour creation, the choice of FIT for setting George up as the *focalizer* (Genette 1980) of the scene is not coincidental, as it forces the reader into George's uncomfortable position by encouraging him or her to engage in role taking to imagine what it must be like to be in that highly embarrassing situation. We may still laugh *at* the protagonist's inappropriate behaviour, but stepping into his shoes can blur the boundary between him and the reader, making it easier for us to feel his discomfort.

The role of free indirect discourse in facilitating empathetic responses or giving readers the impression that they understand the character has been investigated empirically (Hakemulder and Koopman 2010, Bray 2007). While, as Bray (2007) points out, there are non-linguistic factors that can override formal textual features in cueing empathy (like character identification or seriousness of the situation), it is reasonable to suggest that linguistic manipulations of focalization affect our relationships with characters. 'Free indirect discourse', argues Vermeule, 'is one of the major literary techniques that writers use to put pressure on our mind-reading capacities' (2010: 72-3) – it gives us clues that point to the workings of someone else's psyche. The appeal of fiction, Vermeule suggests, is that it gives us access to 'really juicy social information': 'information that it would be too costly, dangerous, and difficult for us to extract from the world on our own' and that uncovers the truth about people's intentions (Vermeule 2010: 14, see also Zunshine 2006 for a similar approach). The allure of cringe humour like that in the wedding speech scene from Haddon's novel, therefore, is threefold. Firstly, it allows us to laugh at the expense of someone who is behaving inappropriately. Secondly, it shows us what happens when social conventions are being infringed in ways that we may not have witnessed in our lives. Thirdly, it enables us to step into the shoes of someone who is transgressing established cultural norms, allowing us to feel the accompanying embarrassment or shame, but feel it in a 'safe' context of an otherwise pleasant, playful humorous narrative world.

Narratives' ability to give us insight into the inner lives of other people can produce powerful emotional effects for readers of comedy. In a novel like *A Spot of Bother*, which relies on narration strategies that expose the thoughts and feelings of its characters, humour is imbued, as one Goodreads reader suggests, with genuine, heartfelt investment in those characters' lives:

> Not so heavy on the punchline but more emphasis on character. It does eventually build up to bombastic farce but even then, it all goes to frame character arcs and the humour is tinged, as is in the whole book, with real heartthumping investment in the welfare of the characters.
> […]
> Massively recommend. You'll laugh. You'll cry. You'll feel queasy. You'll want to call your mum.

As the reader suggests, the 'bombastic farce' to which the story builds – meaning, most likely, the climactic events on George's daughter's wedding day – is not straightforwardly amusing, but rather 'tinged' with feelings for the characters. The novel, according to the reader, will make you 'laugh', 'cry' and 'feel queasy'. The cringe humour cued by the stylistic construction of George's farcical speech scene can be considered one of those moments in which, owing to our investment in the characters, such contrasting emotional reactions are evoked simultaneously. The complex humorous response associated with cringe comedy, therefore, can be viewed as part of the immersive quality of those humorous narratives which encourage us to form feelings for their characters.

4.4. Conclusion

Characterization is a powerful tool in the creation of narrative humour. From humorously manipulating easily accessible stereotypes about people to building on familiar stock types in order to create disruptive misfits, writers of comic narratives rely on a range of techniques to evoke our amusement. This amusement, however, can be destabilized by other character-led emotions triggered in the course of reading. While some characters' 'misfit' qualities allow us to laugh *at* them, the relatability of those constructed as 'everyman' or 'everywoman' can facilitate responses of identification and empathy. These reactions, especially in those instances of narrative humour based on the humorous blunders of comic heroes and heroines, can make the reader open to experiencing uncomfortable, negative emotion. A misfit protagonist is able to shield the reader from the potential negative impact of his or her humorously disruptive behaviour by granting us 'safe' distance from the situation, thus inviting us to see the disruption as humorous. The perceived closeness constructed between the reader and an every(wo)man protagonist, however, can cause us to experience the embarrassment together with the character as well as laugh at their behaviour, leading to the complex humorous response of cringe humour.

5

Reacting to story structures

From the overarching structure of the main story line to the build-up of individual narrative situations, the ordering and structuring of events in comic novels and short stories can both add to the creation of humour and also destabilize comedy by cueing responses unrelated to amusement. In order to control the reader's familiarity with the narrative world, writers of comic narratives employ techniques which manipulate the amount of information readers receive regarding how the story events are likely to develop. For the reader, the levels of awareness about what can be expected to happen in the narrative will determine the reaction to the unfolding plot situations: surprise, suspense or a combination of the two. The emotional reactions of surprise and suspense – integral parts of our experience of humorous worlds – are cued by stylistic manipulations of the presentation of story events. The particular types of story events explored in this chapter are the misfortunes, obstacles and difficulties encountered by characters in comic narratives. Those problems, depending on how quickly they are resolved, can become sources of straightforward amusement, but they can also be made to cue more complex humorous responses in the readers of comic narratives.

5.1. Theoretical background

5.1.1. Plot structures, emotion and expectation

Some of the responses experienced in the course of engaging with narrative texts are evoked by the way stories are told. The recognition that authors manipulate the distribution of information about narrative events when developing their plots is based on the theoretical distinction between the *story* which is being recounted and the *discourse* in which the story is presented to the recipient (Chatman 1978). The storyteller's presentation and ordering of the evens in the plot is a strategy often referred to as *exposition*; narrative texts are systems of expositional gaps which are set up by authors (via narrators), and which force readers to continue posing and answering questions, thus sustaining narrative interest (Sternberg 1978, see also Tan 1994). The enjoyment of being able to fill in the gaps set up by the narrator and the associated emotional reward is said to be strongest in those discourse structures which elicit the emotions of *surprise* and *suspense*, particularly in those stories constructed to lead to a satisfying narrative resolution (Brewer and Lichtenstein 1982). Surprise is elicited when the presentation of new, unexpected information forces us to review our knowledge of the narrative events and form a fresh interpretation of the text (Brewer 1996; Tobin 2009). Suspense is a reaction to a situation which presents us with uncertainty, often created by withholding information about an important outcome (Gerrig 1993; Tan 1994; Brewer 1996). Our interest in narrative outcomes is key to the experience of stories: Allbritton and Gerrig (1991) suggest that our preference for a particular resolution of story events gives rise to patterns of *participatory responses (p-responses)*. P-responses, which include suspense surrounding unknown outcomes, hopes for preferred outcomes, and considering possible alternatives to the actual outcome, arise from our emotional involvement in the plot.

Most written texts, including narratives, are sites for interaction where the writer attempts to meet the reader's needs by anticipating what the reader may be expecting – reading seems in fact to be based on continuously forming expectations or hypotheses which are either supported or refuted (Hoey 2001). That occurs on two levels, where some of the reader's questions are more immediate than others – our expectations about the immediately unfolding text are formulated at the same time as the larger-scale hypotheses about the text as a whole. Hoey (2001) ties large-scale expectations about the development of the text to the idea of genre, suggesting that the 'regularity of patterning' in genres means that, on the basis of other texts of the same type, we have grown to expect certain features. With regard to narratives specifically, the two additional techniques which, as Hoey suggests, help the reader form predictions about how the text will unfold are *previews* (statements which signal the nature of the text to the reader) and *intertextuality* (the way the understanding of the text is affected by other, previous texts). In many narratives, genre signals, preview statements and intertextuality cues can lead the reader to formulate assumptions about how the plot will develop.

5.1.2. Humour studies approaches to plot structures in comedy

One of the most recognizable features of a comic plot is the occurrence of individual humorous episodes, such as comic events and gags, which are interspersed throughout the narrative. In reference to film and television comedy, Neale and Krutnik (1990) define *comic events* as humorous forms which can be more or less integral to the structure of the plot, with some that are essential to the development of the story, and some which are of no narrative consequence. A comic event, crucially, is an instance of humour in which action and dialogue are combined – unlike a *gag*, which is 'non-linguistic comic action' linked primarily to the domain of the visual and the physical (Neale and Krutnik 1990: 51). Like jokes or wisecracks, comic events and gags are forms of immediately recognizable humour constructed so as to trigger amusement, and as such, they rely on an easily resolvable humorous incongruity. A key stage in our resolution of this incongruity is surprise – in fact, as Neale and Krutnik suggest, all humour-inducing components of comic plots are fundamentally dependent on surprise.

One feature of comic events and gags is their recurrence in the plot of a comic narrative: a *running gag*, for example, is a term for when the same gag or its variations are interspersed throughout the story (Neale and Krutnik 1990). Research in comic narratives emphasizes the importance of repetition as a structural feature of humorous texts. In her comprehensive account of humorous short stories, Ermida (2008) suggests that 'recurrence' is one of the essential principles which the narrative has to obey in order to be classified as humorous – a narrative which does not exhibit recurrence, therefore, cannot be considered humorous. Attardo (2002: 236), whose main focus is on the humorous lines which occur in comic narratives, outlines a number of ways in which individual lines show similarity to each other: a strand, for example, is a pattern of related lines (e.g. lines targeting a particular character) which can run through a passage, while a bridge is when such related lines occur far from each other. Triezenberg (2004, 2008) sees repetition as one of the *humour enhancers* used by writers of comic narratives to alert the reader that the text is to be interpreted as humorous. Recurrence in comic texts, therefore, can be said to magnify the humour of gags and other comic structures, bring out the humour in elements not inherently humorous, as well as signal to the receiver that the text is to be perceived as comic.

While recurring, surprising comic events help to inject humour into comedy, another distinguishing feature of comic narratives is an overarching trajectory of the plot that leads, through numerous obstacles, to a happy ending. Just like a short humorous form relies on an immediate resolution of incongruity, so does the extended comic narrative rely on a more encompassing resolution of plot events. A positive, satisfying conclusion to a story is a feature that distinguishes comedy from tragedy – a comic ending is one where, after a string of complications, the original status quo is restored (Frye 1957).

5.2. *Stabilizing cues*: Expecting the unexpected

Many of the comic events that help to establish the plot as humorous are built around obstacles and misfortunes which cause problems for characters, but which are presented to readers as amusing complications.

Even though readers of humorous texts are often cued to anticipate such complications in the course of the plot, the humorous quality of characters' failures and setbacks lies in the surprise they can trigger and the resolution of that surprise once we realize that the problematic event has a humorous quality to it. The predictability of the overall structure of the comic plot (where, typically, a series of obstacles is followed by a happy ending) does not diminish the surprise, but protects us from the negative emotional impact that negative plot outcomes could otherwise evoke.

5.2.1. Foreshadowing: Setting an expectation of comedy

The role of expectation in our experience of comedy cannot be overstated. The openings of many comic narratives, therefore, contain cues which give readers a clear indication about the type of story they can anticipate, and how the plot is likely to develop. Below are extracts from the beginning of *A Short History of Tractors in Ukrainian*, which openly signal how the narrative will unfold:

Example 30

I
Two phone calls and a funeral

[…]
It all started with a phone call.

My father's voice, quavery with excitement, crackles down the line. 'Good news, Nadezhda. I'm getting married!'
[…]
'But Pappa, have you really thought this through? It seems very sudden. I mean, she must be a lot younger than you.'
I modulate my voice carefully, to conceal any signs of disapproval, like a worldy-wise adult dealing with a love-struck adolescent.
'Thirty-six. She's thirty-six and I'm eighty-four. So what?' (He pronounces 'vat'.)
There is a snap in his voice. He has anticipated this question.

'Well, it's quite an age difference...'
'Nadezhda, I never thought you would be so bourgeois.' (He puts emphasis on the last syllable – wah!)
'No, no.' He has me on the defensive. 'It's just that ... there could be problems.'
There will be no problems, says Pappa. He has anticipated all problems. [...]

(Lewycka [2005] 2006: 1–2)

The opening of the novel is highly evocative of a comic plot. Not only does it contain a characterization strategy where a sympathetic, ordinary protagonist (Nadezhda) is set in opposition to a volatile, eccentric misfit (father), but the title of the chapter is a clear reference to the comedy classic *Four Weddings and a Funeral* (1994, dir. Mike Newell). The reference functions as a nod towards those viewers who are familiar with the film and an indication that, like the film, the novel will also involve multiple complications, the majority of them humorous, some of them tragic. Most interesting, however, are the preview statements (Hoey 2001) interspersed through the opening paragraphs. On the first page of the novel, we are already given a clear indication that the main source of complications in the narrative will be an elderly man's snap decision to marry a virtually unknown young woman. This alone could be enough to cue the reader to expect trouble later on in a way which can be linked to *foreshadowing* (e.g. Chatman 1978), that is, the scattering of minor plot events that helps the reader infer how the narrative will develop. What stands out in the opening of *A Short History* is the repetition of the word 'problems', which implies that the narrator is aware of the turn which the events are likely to take. Nadezhda's tentative 'It's just that ... there could be problems.' helps the reader articulate his or her own expectations regarding the development of the story, indicating that there will be problems on the way. The character's father, it appears, 'has anticipated' not only his daughter's (and the reader's) reservations, but also potential problems. The readers, however, are encouraged to side with the sympathetic comic protagonist, bracing themselves for a plot full of amusing complications.

5.2.2. Complication: Generating amusing problems

We expect the above complications to be amusing because of the generic, intertextuality and mode/mood cues which prepare us for processing a comic plot. While 'complication' is a general label which applies to most narratives to mean 'an event or series of events which are unexpected, dangerous, or in general unusual' and often have negative consequences that demand a narrative resolution (van Dijk 1975: 289), here I concentrate on *humorous complications* specifically, and on their *humorous resolution* which allows us to 'reframe' the problem as humorous. Rather than appealing to our emotional engagement by triggering participatory responses (Allbritton and Gerrig 1991, discussed previously), the role of a humorous complication is to evoke amusement.

Humorous complications, in the way in which they are approached here, will be linked to the notions of *comic events* and *gags* outlined by Neale and Krutnik (1990) in relation to film and television comedy. In a multimodal comic text, a comic event is a humorous form integral to the framework of the narrative – it is, as Neale and Krutnik point out, 'a consequence of the existence of characters and a plot' (1990: 44). Comic events can be more or less integral to the structure of the plot, with some that are essential to the development of the story, and some which are of no narrative consequence (Neale and Krutnik 1990: 45). A comic event, crucially, is an instance of humour in which action and dialogue are combined – unlike a *gag*, which Neale and Krutnik define as 'non-linguistic comic action' and link primarily to the domain of the visual and the physical (1990: 51). A gag, which, like a comic event, can be either an integral piece of the narrative structure, or an (often gratuitous) digression that interrupts the plot, relies on surprise for its humorous effect. More developed forms referred to as *articulated gags* work by producing unexpected variations on a single action or a series of actions, where an action is led to take an unexpected turn by going against a sociocultural norm or a pre-established narrative expectation (Neale and Krutnik 1990: 53).

Chosen aspects of both comic events and gags, despite their primary relevance to multimodal media texts, can be applied to the humorous story structures which are integral to written humorous narratives. The following extract from Helen Fielding's *Bridget Jones's Diary* is an example of a humorous complication which combines features of a comic event and a gag:

> **Example 31**
>
> At that moment the phone rang. It was the mini-cab firm the girls had rung half an hour earlier saying there'd been a terrible multiple pile-up in Ladbroke Grove, plus all their cars had unexpectedly exploded and they weren't going to be able to come for another three hours.
>
> (Fielding [1996] 1998: 128)

Like a gag, this complication interrupts the plot in a surprising way. The surprise, while based partly on the abruptness of the phone call itself, stems mainly from the exaggerated nature of the event which seemingly caused the phone exchange – like in an articulated gag, we are presented with multiple incidents (a pile-up, car explosions) which form a series of related actions. The disruption provided by these actions is not strictly a mere digression (it has minor consequences for the characters whose cab is delayed), but it is relatively gratuitous in that it is not essential to the development of the plot. Despite the visual character of the complication triggered by the images of cars crashing and exploding, the centrality of the telephone conversation makes it difficult to classify the event as a 'non-linguistic comic action', therefore it may be more appropriate to refer to it as a comic event rather than a gag.

Relating the complications of written comedy to similar plot structures found in other texts allows us to situate the term 'humorous complication' alongside those already established in the study of narrative humour. It does not, however, necessarily explain why those structures can evoke amusement. In what follows, I focus on the notion of *surprise* to explore the amusing potential of humorous complications, which are defined as:

> A **humorous complication** in the written narrative context is a surprising event which has a negative, sometimes very serious,

consequence for one or more of the characters, but which is presented as humorous to the reader. It is a situation that (a) is based around a problem which (b) contains unexpected, incongruous qualities and which (c) swiftly reaches a **humorous resolution** once the reader is able to distance him- or herself from the seriousness of the problem.

The emphasis on surprise and a fast humorous resolution allow problematic plot events to trigger amusement instead of more serious emotional engagement. In a playful, non-serious humorous narrative context, we anticipate that events will go humorously wrong, but we want those humorous complications to take us by surprise.

As far as text organization is concerned, such a problem-based course of events can be linked to what Hoey calls the *Problem-Solution pattern*, which leads our lower-level expectations regarding how the immediately unfolding text will develop. The easily recognizable, culturally popular Problem-Solution pattern is composed of the stages of *Situation, Problem, Response* and *Evaluation/Result* (2001: 123). Its key element, according to Hoey, is the question 'What did you do about it?' which the reader asks after finding out that an agent encountered a Problem. The following Response should lead to a Result. While Hoey's Problem-Solution pattern of text organization places emphasis on the Response (doing something about the problem that arose), its humour-specific equivalent seems to concentrate on the Problem itself. Instead of asking 'What did you do about the Problem?', we are more interested to know 'What went wrong?' In the humorous context where we are striving for events to spin amusingly out of control but have been given no cues as to how and when that will happen, encountering an unexpected problem triggers satisfying surprise. The problem, importantly, does not need to be solved – in the minicab extract (Example 31), our amusement is likely to be triggered exclusively by the unfortunate event, independent of how the characters responded to fix the situation.

For the reader of a humorous narrative, the humorous resolution of a surprise at an unexpected and problematic plot event stems not from observing the negative situation reach a positive solution, but from shifting our perspective of the situation itself – noticing its humorous side. The key here is the reader's recognition that the complication, despite causing problems for the characters, is in fact part of a larger humorous framework and it can therefore be treated as humorous, not threatening. It is particularly clear in the above passage from *Bridget Jones*, where our potential puzzlement at the surprisingly exaggerated nature of the incident, when contrasted with our real-world preconceptions of the reliability of minicabs (in the British context, at least), can lead us to reach a conclusion that the narrative complication was created to cause our amusement, not concern.

That kind of puzzlement-humorous conclusion pattern can be seen to correspond with the incongruity-resolution approach to humour appreciation, where emphasis is placed on the surprising nature of a humorous stimulus and the resolution of this surprise as a source of humour. According to Suls' classic model (1972), surprise is a response which follows from encountering an incongruous humorous stimulus, and which precedes the cognitive work necessary to resolve the incongruity. The surprise stage, therefore, can be considered a crucial element of processing a humorous, problem-based situation. Drawing on Hoey's (2001) Problem-Solution pattern and Suls' (1972) incongruity-resolution model, the full structure of a humorous complication can thus be summarized as: *[situation], problem, surprise, humorous resolution, [amusement]*. The problem, which may be preceded by a description of the situation, can be seen as a humorous stimulus that triggers surprise and, if successfully – humorously – resolved, can lead to amusement.

To illustrate this process in more detail, below I show how a very serious problem which concerns a highly sympathetic protagonist can be manipulated to become a humorous complication. The following humorous complication revolves around a problem which, unlike the comparatively trivial minicab delay in Example 30, has serious repercussions for the narrative's protagonist. In the extract below, Arthur Dent, the hero of *The Hitchhiker's Guide to the Galaxy*, explains to his local council worker that he received very little notice about the fact that his house had been scheduled to be demolished:

Example 32

The first thing I knew about it was when a workman arrived at my home yesterday. I asked him if he'd come to clean the windows and he said no he'd come to demolish the house. He didn't tell me straight away, of course. Oh no. First he wiped a couple of windows and charged me a fiver. Then he told me.

(Adams [1979] 2002: 7)

The situation described in the passage can be viewed as a humorous complication because it is based around a problem, and the problem is constructed to feature incongruous qualities which evoke surprise. Rather unexpectedly, it turns out that the worker who first informed Arthur about the demolition of the house was posing as a window cleaner to make some money on the side. This unexpected detail about the worker's conduct is very far removed from what could be expected in a typical situation of this kind, and therefore its appearance creates a surprising, incongruous effect. In a narrative world which is otherwise humorous, the incorporation of this incongruous quality into our interpretation of the problem is likely to lead to a humorous resolution.

With regard to style, what stands out is the chatty, informal register which does not seem to match the seriousness of the situation – the sentence 'First he wiped a couple of windows and charged me a fiver.' seems particularly nonchalant, suggesting the speaker's surprisingly non-committal, casual attitude to what happened to him. Another technique which can potentially distance us from the events described is the use of parallel structures. The construction of 'I asked him if he'd come to clean the windows and he said no he'd come to demolish the house.' stands out due to the seemingly unnecessary repetition of the unit 'he'd come to', which appears twice in the short sentence. This noticeable structural parallelism can draw our attention to the linguistic layer of the text, shifting that attention away from the actual story events. It is worth pointing out again that there is nothing inherently humorous about either foregrounding techniques or informal register, as they appear in both comic and non-comic texts. However, in a larger humorous context they can act as distancing devices which complement other stabilizing cues, such as the problem-surprise-humorous resolution pattern discussed above.

A humorous resolution occurs when detecting an unexpected incongruity in some part of the description of the problem encourages us to reframe our perception of those aspects of the complication as humorous. Example 32 offers two sources of this kind of incongruity. Firstly, the surprising detail about the worker's window-cleaning fraud stands out as inappropriate, or incongruous, in the situation. Secondly, the main character's matter-of-fact description of the problematic event clashes with what could otherwise be expected from someone in that position. By being surprised by those incongruous qualities of the event, we are reminded that the narrative world in which we are immersed is a humorous one – one which, as one reader suggests in his Goodreads review of *The Hitchhiker's Guide*, is based on 'ridiculous plotting':

> Since I was maybe twelve or thirteen when I read this, I'm sure some of the dry humor flew right over my head, but the slapstick, sight gags, and ridiculous plotting sure didn't. There are so many absurdist details in this ricocheting narrative that presenting you with a thorough summary would be tough.

Adams' novel, as the reader points out, abounds in various types of humorous complications. Some of them, although intended to amuse (e.g. gags or slapstick), may not follow a clear-cut problem-surprise-humorous resolution pattern. Generally, however, what distinguishes a comic complication from a non-comic one is some incongruous, surprising quality of the problem and the humorous resolution we reach once we reframe it in accordance with the overall humorous mode of the narrative.

5.2.3. Resolution: Leading to a happy ending

One reason why the problems which lead to humorous complications tend to be perceived as non-threatening is that our large-scale expectation of comic narratives is one of an overall comic resolution – a happy ending. There may be obstacles on the way, but they, as Frye suggests, simply 'form the action of the comedy', and it is the overcoming of them that leads to the comic resolution (1957: 164). This expectation that, despite complications, everything will be 'alright' in the end, can protect the reader from the potential negative impact of problematic story events. While this will not be true of all comic narratives (as I outline further), it is most likely to apply to the sub-genre of romantic comedy, which, as Frye points out in relation to its origins as the New Comedy of the classical period, culminates in a highly manipulated twist in the plot 'which is the comic form of Aristotle's "discovery"' (1957: 44). The low mimetic New Comedy, which centres around an intrigue between a young couple whose happiness is blocked by some kind of opposition, ends in a twist that allows for the characters to be united and accepted by the society.

This formula can still be found in contemporary romantic comedies, including *Bridget Jones's Diary* and *High Fidelity* analysed here. Both texts involve highly identifiable, ordinary protagonists faced with obstacles which stand in the way of them being united with their romantic interest. To the joy of their friends and families (and, most likely, the reader), they do eventually find their way back to their partners. In both cases, the positive change of fortune has an element of surprise to it and is more or less out of the protagonist's hands. Rob's ex-girlfriend Laura unexpectedly recommences their relationship after her father's funeral, and then subsequently surprises Rob even more by organizing a big party for him, which allows for their local community to come together in a happy ending. Bridget, in an even more dramatic finale, is swept off her feet by Mark, who appears during Christmas lunch at her parents' not only to finally confess his love for Bridget, but also to rescue the family from an inebriated Portuguese conman who attempts to elope with Bridget's mother. Both *Bridget Jones's Diary* and

High Fidelity end in a plot twist which brings about a restoration of the desired status quo – in other words, a comic resolution.

5.3. *Destabilizing cues*: Bearing the unbearable

Narrative comedy relies on stylistic techniques that turn problematic plot events into sources of amusing surprise. Many humorous complications, however, will be structured so as to retain some of their negative emotional impact and trigger responses unrelated to amusement, thus destabilizing our experience of comedy.

5.3.1. Enhancing involvement in the plot

The humorous complications which drive comic plots, despite being framed as amusing for the reader's benefit, are adverse events which often have profound repercussions for the characters involved in them. 'The important thing to understand,' suggests comedy writer Jonathan Lynn, 'is that the events of the comedy are deadly serious and potentially tragic *for the characters*. If they are not sufficiently important, the audience may feel that its time has been wasted' (2011: 5–6). The audience's interest in the plot, therefore, is partly dependent on the seriousness of the potential *outcomes* faced by the characters. In their discussion of readers' involvement in texts, Allbritton and Gerrig (1991) distinguish between *positive* and *negative outcomes* for characters, which give rise to *positive* or *negative preferences* in readers. Positive preferences are those where the reader is hoping for a positive outcome – an outcome that would be considered desirable outside the context of the story. Negative preferences, on the other hand, are associated with hoping for negative outcomes – ones which would typically be considered undesirable (Allbritton and Gerrig suggest 'a successful killing' as an example). Those preferences give rise to patterns of participatory responses (p-responses), which are readers' reactions 'that arise as a consequence of involvement in the text' (Allbritton and Gerrig 1991: 603).

The concept of p-responses was subsequently developed by Gerrig (1993), who stressed their noninferential nature (as opposed to the logical, knowledge-based inferencing we use to 'bridge gaps' in texts, Gerrig 1993: 27) and outlined *hopes and preferences, replotting* and *suspense* as the three types of such noninferential responses. Hopes and preferences are most closely tied to Allbritton and Gerrig's original notion of readers hoping for particular outcomes, giving rise to positive or negative preferences. Gerrig stresses, however, that while in real-life situations positive preferences tend to be the norm, in the context of a particular narrative readers can be cued to prefer either kind of outcome (1993: 71). That, as I have already signalled (and will discuss further), is particularly true of humorous narratives, where readers are often encouraged to strive for unfortunate, problematic, unsuccessful events which could be considered negative outcomes, since those outcomes are comically presented for us as humorous complications. While hopes and preferences are responses which we formulate before we discover narrative outcomes, replotting is a reaction which can occur once those outcomes are revealed to us. Replotting involves mentally commenting on the resolution of events, considering possible alternatives to the actual outcome. It is easiest to observe, Gerrig suggests, when the outcome has been particularly negative (1993: 90). The final type of p-response, suspense, is the expression of uncertainty which surrounds an unknown outcome. Its vital component is the period of delay between the point when suspense is initiated and the point when the outcome is revealed. Suspense is the one p-response which will be discussed further in more detail, as its role in film and television comedy has received attention in humour studies (Neale and Krutnik 1990: 55–6; King 2002: 49), and the findings are highly relevant to written humorous narratives.

(i) Suspense
Suspense as a reaction to story structures is associated with a delayed revelation of an important plot outcome. In his approach to suspense

as one of the p-responses which accompany processing narrative texts, Gerrig (1993) defines it as follows:

> The experience of suspense should occur when a reader (1) lacks knowledge about (2) some sufficiently important target outcome. Feelings of suspense will be heightened to the extent that (3) the target outcome maps out a challenging problem space and (4) the author is able to sustain participatory responses over a period of delay.
>
> (Gerrig 1993: 79)

Suspense is achieved when the reader is led to wait for an important outcome, and this wait is a source of uncomfortable tension. Its close association with discomfort makes suspense far removed from the positive emotion of amusement, suggesting that the creation of suspense has very little in common with the creation of humour. Douglas Adams plays with this idea in *The Hitchhiker's Guide to the Galaxy*, where on one occasion he makes a point out of protecting his reader from the uncomfortable feeling of suspense. The example, which appears as the characters' space ship approaches an unknown planet (which may or may not be Magrathea, the planet that they are looking for), is particularly useful as it shows the inner workings of narrative suspense, as well as commenting on its experience for the reader:

Example 33

Stress and nervous tension are now serious social problems in all parts of the Galaxy, and it is in order that this situation should not be in any way exacerbated that the following facts will now be revealed in advance.

The planet in question *is* in fact the legendary Magrathea.

The deadly missile attack shortly to be launched by an ancient automatic defence system will result merely in the breakage of three cups and a mousecage, the bruising of somebody's upper arm, and the untimely creation and sudden demise of a bowl of petunias and an innocent sperm whale.

In order that some sense of mystery should still be preserved, no revelation will yet be made concerning whose upper arm sustains the bruise. This fact may safely be made the subject of suspense since it is of no significance whatsoever.

(Adams [1979] 2002: 103)

The narrator, seemingly mindful of the negative emotional effects of suspense, reveals the outcomes of the characters' arrival at Magrathea, so as to spare the reader the tension. However, despite this apparent concern for the reader's feelings, suspenseful events do abound in the plot of *The Hitchhiker's Guide*, which frequently leads us to wait for the outcomes of significant events. Adams' book, part comic novel, part science-fiction cliff-hanger, shows how one text can incorporate elements of both humour and suspense. The example above illustrates one of the possible uses of suspense for humour creation, but this type of a humorous deconstruction is by no means a common technique in comic novels and short stories. More typically, suspense and amusement are cued simultaneously in a complex humorous response, resulting in what will be referred to as *comic suspense*.

(ii) Comic suspense

Comic suspense occurs when amusement and suspense are triggered together, creating a blend of uncomfortable tension and humorous enjoyment. Its main ingredients are *predictability* and *delay*: a narrative situation involving comic suspense will be structured to cue an expectation of a particular course of events, but will delay the revelation of how these events actually develop. This approach to suspense in humorous narratives is informed by King's (2002) work on film comedy, where the tension associated with comic suspense is said to lie in the gap between our knowledge that something is about to go wrong and the 'delayed revelation of what *exactly* will go wrong in any particular case' (King 2002: 49). In other words, we have been cued to predict that something in the narrative world is about to go wrong, but we are made to wait to find out what it is and how exactly it will happen. As Neale and Krutnik suggest in relation to film and television comedy, 'If there is a banana skin around, *someone* will fall on it' (1990: 55) – the source of tension is the delayed revelation of who it is and in what circumstances.

The following example from David Sedaris' 'A Learning Curve' illustrates this phenomenon. In the autobiographical short story, Sedaris recounts his suspenseful first class as a creative writing tutor – a job which he had been eagerly looking forward to, but for which he failed to adequately prepare. Based on his idea of what teachers do, he focused his preparations on finding the right briefcase and cutting leaf-shaped name tags out of orange paper. As a result, he arrives in the classroom with a professional-looking briefcase filled with nothing but paper leaves and pins, which he accordingly distributes to the students:

Example 34

'All right then,' I said. 'Okay, here we go.' I opened my briefcase and realized that I'd never thought beyond this moment. The orange leaves were the extent of my lesson plan, but still I searched the empty briefcase, mindful that I had stupidly armed my audience with straight pins. I guess I'd been thinking that, without provocation, my students would talk, offering their thoughts and opinions on the issues of the day. I'd imagined myself sitting on the edge of the desk, overlooking a forest of raised hands. The students would simultaneously shout to be heard, and I'd pound on something in order to silence them. 'Whoa people,' I'd yell. 'Calm down, you'll all get your turn. One at a time, one at a time.'

The error of my thinking yawned before me. A terrible silence overtook the room, and seeing no other option, I instructed my students to pull out their notebooks and write a brief essay related to the theme of profound disappointment.

(Sedaris [2000] 2002: 85)

We knew that David was unprepared to teach and expected that things would go wrong for him – what we did not know was *how*. The opening of the passage ('"All right then," I said. "Okay, here we go." I opened my briefcase and realized that I'd never thought beyond this moment.') confirms our overall expectations regarding the course of events (that is, David will fail), but sets a new question, which can be summarized as 'How much worse will it get before it gets better?' Being familiar with the general humorous context of Sedaris' writing helps to view the uncomfortable situation as a source of amusement rather than of genuine risk for the character, but it does not mean that we do not anticipate the unpleasantness of the situation to exacerbate. On the contrary, we suspect (and possibly dread the fact) that the situation will be getting worse, but the revelation of how bad exactly is being delayed.

Rather than immediately show the reader how David resolves the problem, the narrator first shifts the perspective from the actual situation of the classroom to the imagined classroom which David envisaged when he was preparing for his first class. This shift is marked by the aspect which suddenly switches from the past simple to past perfect ('I'd been thinking', 'I'd imagined'), and by the subjunctive mood which changes the focus from David's reality to his imaginary first class ('I'd pound', 'I'd yell'). This process can be linked to what Emmott (1997) calls a *frame switch*, as it is a situation where the reader's attention is led to move from one context to another. The contexts, although different in that one is real and one is imagined, refer to the same situation; David's first class. As a result, the reader, although potentially distracted by the exaggerated qualities of the idyllic imagined scene, is being kept aware that a *frame recall* (Emmott 1997) is about to follow, in which we return to the original context and the outcome will finally be revealed. The comic suspense in the extract, therefore, relies on the narrator suspending the events in one narrative context (or *frame*, Emmott 1997) and forcing the reader to switch to a different context to wait for a resolution. That resolution is provided when, after a period of delay, David finally suggests an activity to the students. The outcome of his first teaching experience, as expected, is a disappointing one – as emphasized by the theme of his proposed assignment. It is important to note that the protagonist, although previously blissfully unaware of how inadequate his preparation had been, realizes his imminent failure soon after the class begins. This means that the reader is likely to experience what Smith (2000: 20) calls *shared suspense* – suspense which, thanks to the insight into the character's mental state (here enabled by first-person narration), the reader shares with the character.

Although the outcome of David's first creative writing class is arguably negative, it has a humorous quality to it. At the heart of this humour lies the surprising, unexpectedly relevant topic of the activity he finally proposes to his students. By asking them to write 'a brief essay related to the theme of profound disappointment', the narrator unexpectedly sums up his own feelings about his first teaching experience, providing what can be considered a punch line to the whole episode. The surprise potentially triggered by that punch line can provide the kind of humorous resolution which, as previously outlined in the discussion of humorous complications, allows us to humorously reframe David's failure by turning something unfortunate into something amusing. While the passage, due to its delayed presentation of the outcome, relies on suspense, it also possesses qualities of a surprising, amusing humorous complication. The inextricable relationship between surprise and amusement means that humorous plot events which have been structured to evoke amusement are likely to rely on surprise. That is why many instances of comic suspense (like Example 34 above) will, after a period of delay, culminate in a moment of amusement-inducing surprise.

In the context of narrative comedy, suspense and surprise are closely linked. The previous section introduced the term 'humorous complication' as a surprise-inducing problem-based plot event and emphasized its reliance on unexpectedness and a swift humorous resolution which helps us view the problem in an amusing light. Instances of comic suspense, by contrast, were said to differ from humorous complications in their reliance on predictability and a delayed revelation of a significant outcome – a slow narrative resolution (narrative resolution here simply means the presentation of the narrative outcome rather than the humorous 'reframing' discussed in relation to humorous complications.) This clear distinction between unpredictability/fast resolution in surprise-based comic events and predictability/slow resolution in suspense-based ones has been outlined by Neale and Krutnik (1990), who discuss it in relation to cinematic gags. A gag which involves suspense, they argue, delays the introduction of the comic event, 'while the narration provides the information necessary to generate anticipation, or slowly unfolds the events with which it will culminate' (Neale and Krutnik 1990: 57). A gag of surprise, however, is structured so that the comic event will be unexpected and it will be presented as quickly as possible (Neale and Krutnik 1990: 56). To return to the banana skin analogy – surprise is triggered once someone unexpectedly slips on one which we did not know was there, and suspense occurs when we are made to wait for someone to slip on one which we have been shown. Despite this apparent contrast between suspense- and surprise-based gags, however, Neale and Krutnik point out that even a comedy which depends on suspense will usually at some point also involve surprise (Neale and Krutnik 1990: 40). A scene which consists of nothing but a banana skin on which someone *may* fall, although potentially suspenseful, has little to do with humour. Amusement is most likely to occur once someone finally falls on the skin, and falls in an unexpected manner that triggers humorous surprise.

5.3.2. Manipulating degrees of knowledge

In order to fully appreciate the blend of suspense and amusement, the reader needs to be led to wait for an outcome which is expected to be negative, but the details of the outcome must come as a surprise. Despite the element of surprise which accompanies the presentation of a negative outcome, comic suspense involves a degree of predictability, ensured by the writer's ability to signal that something is about to go wrong. In other words, we must be provided with some form of awareness that a complication is about to occur, but with incomplete knowledge of the actual nature of the complication. This kind of withholding of knowledge (from the reader, but also from the characters), is a technique which allows writers to manipulate our reactions to suspenseful plot events in narrative comedy.

(i)   Dramatic irony

'In comedy,' suggests writer Jonathan Lynn, 'the more information the audience has about a scene and the less information one or

more of the characters in the scene has, the funnier it will be'
(Lynn 2011: 168). The device which allows for such a distribution
of knowledge is *dramatic irony*, which is when the audience knows
something that a character does not. Aside from its use in humour
creation, dramatic irony can be found in texts which involve
suspense, making it particularly useful in the construction of comic
suspense. With reference to film comedy, King (2002: 48) uses the
phrase 'differential hierarchies of knowledge' to describe how the
concealment of information from the viewer can lead to different
effects than the concealment of information from characters. While
the withholding of information from the viewer (or the viewer and
the character together), as King suggests, can result in a moment
of comic surprise when the truth is revealed, concealment from
characters within the narrative is often used to create comic suspense
(2002: 48). It is this second type of withholding that forms a gap
between the knowledge of the reader and the knowledge of the
characters, and consequently produces dramatic irony.

The following example from P. G. Wodehouse's *Right Ho, Jeeves*
(Example 35) illustrates how dramatic irony can be used for comic
effect, where the reader is made to writhe in anticipation of a humorous
disaster – a disaster which the reader can clearly foresee, but to which
the characters are oblivious. The extract comes from a long scene in
which the protagonist and first-person narrator Bertie Wooster makes
an attempt at match-making, hoping to help Gussie Fink-Nottle unite
with the woman of his dreams, Miss Bassett. Gussie is too shy to confess
his love to Miss Bassett, and so Bertie invites her out for a walk to fill
her in on the situation. Unfortunately, in his effort to create an air of
mystery and romance, Bertie inadvertently leads Miss Bassett up the
wrong path. 'It may interest you,' he begins, 'that there is an aching heart
at Brinkley Court' (Wodehouse [1934] 2008: 112). After a prolonged
exchange in which, to Bertie's irritation, Miss Bassett is trying to guess
whom Bertie is referring to as the 'aching heart' (there are a number
of young couples at Brinkley Court), she seems to finally grasp what
Bertie is trying to say:

Example 35

'Oh, Mr Wooster!'

'I take it you believe in love at first sight?'

'I do, indeed.'

'Well, that's what happened to this aching heart. It fell in love at first sight, and ever since it's been eating itself out, as I believe the expression is.'

There was a silence. She had turned away and was watching a duck out on the lake. It was tucking into weeds, a thing I've never been able to understand anyone wanting to do. Though I suppose, if you face it squarely, they're no worse than spinach. She stood drinking it in for a bit, and then it suddenly stood on its head and disappeared, and this seemed to break the spell.

'Oh, Mr Wooster!' she said again, and from the tone of her voice, I could see that I had got her going.

(Wodehouse [1934] 2008: 113)

Familiarity with the narrative world and its multiple humorous complications may have led some readers to suspect that Bertie's scheme would backfire from the moment he invited Miss Bassett for a walk to inform her about Gussie's affection. The extract above, however, provides an indication as to *how exactly* the plan will fail: Miss Bassett misinterprets Bertie's indirectness and romantic register to conclude that *Bertie* is confessing his love to her. Her sudden speechlessness, broken only by an occasional exclamation of 'Oh, Mr Wooster!', and the fact that she turns away from him to ponder on his words are signals that she has made up her mind as to who the 'aching heart' is and whom it is aching for. Bertie, however, seems perfectly unaware of what Miss Bassett is thinking – in fact, he seems convinced that his match-making scheme is unfolding well.

This disparity between Bertie's and Miss Bassett's contrasting interpretations of the same event is communicated through the combination of direct speech between the characters (the meaning of which is left to the reader's judgement) and Bertie's free direct thought (in which he comments on what he believes to be happening, but which clashes with the reader's position). Our direct access to Bertie's thoughts – and the textual cues which allow us to evaluate those thoughts as erroneous – give an impression of what one Goodreads reader of Wodehouse refers to as 'Bertie's voice':

> Bertie's voice in the Jeeves books is one of the greatest achievements in all of comic fiction—absolutely consistent, totally confident, unerringly wrong.

The reader's interpretation of Bertie's voice as 'unerringly wrong' suggests that readers of Wodehouse's *Jeeves and Wooster* narratives, including *Right Ho, Jeeves*, are very aware of the gap between their own knowledge and the knowledge of the character.

Right Ho, Jeeves's Miss Bassett finally reveals her interpretation of Bertie Wooster's words – and indeed the suspicions she had held for a longer time. By clarifying the miscommunication and putting an end to Bertie's ignorance, she provides a solution to the problem which had been the source of suspense. Up to this point, we have been experiencing suspense *on behalf* of Bertie, who himself was oblivious to the situation until the very last moment. While the revelation of the outcome relieves the reader of one type of discomfort, we are soon faced with another, this time one which we share with the protagonist. As it turns out, Miss Bassett thinks that Bertie is proposing to her, but instead of directly giving him the answer, she babbles on, keeping him and the reader in suspense as to what her response will be. Unlike the example from Sedaris (Example 34), in which the suspense was condensed in a short paragraph with a surprising 'punch line' resolution, here the suspense is much more prolonged, and the surprise more subtle. Our privileged position of knowledge made possible through dramatic irony makes it easier to anticipate how exactly the events will go wrong, therefore maximizing the suspense and minimizing the surprise. Rather than leading to the 'ha-ha' moment which results from a comic resolution of surprise in more straightforward humorous complications, here we are faced with a few 'oh-no' moments which precede imminent (humorous) disaster, as the writer cues us to join the dots before the characters do.

(ii) Recurrence

Aside from giving us direct access to the protagonist's thoughts and allowing us to see that he is misinterpreting the situation, Wodehouse's other strategy for creating dramatic irony is the use of *recurrence* as a structural technique. One of the reasons why we knew that Bertie's plan would backfire is that we have been given sufficient information about the outcomes of his previous schemes – as valet Jeeves very politely sums it up in a conversation with Bertie which precedes the Miss Bassett match-making fiasco, 'Well, sir, if I may take the liberty of reminding you of it, your plans in the past have not always been uniformly successful' (Wodehouse [1934] 2008: 91). Bertie Wooster's failed schemes thus become a recurring theme in the novel, making it possible for the reader familiar with the narrative world to guess their outcomes before the character does.

Research on comic narratives emphasizes the importance of recurrence as a structural feature of comedy texts. In her comprehensive account of humorous short stories, Ermida (2008: 172–3) suggests that *Principle of Recurrence* is one of the essential principles which the narrative has to obey in order to be classified as humorous – a narrative which does not exhibit recurrence, therefore, cannot be considered humorous. Nash (1985: 72–3) proposes the notion of a *root joke* which, through recurrent mention, informs the infrastructure of a comic narrative (like the circular logic of Catch-22 frequently mentioned in Heller's novel). Attardo (2002: 236), whose main focus is on the humorous *jab lines* which occur in comic narratives, outlines a number of ways in which individual lines show similarity to each other: a *strand*, for example, is a pattern of related lines (e.g. lines targeting a particular character) which can run through a passage, while a *bridge* is when such related lines occur far from each other. Triezenberg (2004, 2008) sees recurrence, which she refers to as *repetition and variation*, as one of the humour enhancers used by writers of comic narratives – techniques which are not funny in themselves, but which alert the reader that the text is to be interpreted as humorous. She suggests that 'repetition with skillful variation allows an author to use the same joke over and over again, magnifying it each time and also impressing the audience with his inventiveness' (Triezenberg 2008: 539). This technique can be seen as the literary equivalent of the film and television-based device called a *running gag*, where the same gag or its variations are interspersed throughout the whole story (Neale and Krutnik 1990: 53). Stand-up comedy makes use of a similar mechanism – comedian Stewart Lee outlines the device referred to as a *callback*, which is when 'the mere reincorporation of an idea from earlier in the set can seem funny in and of itself, if its re-emergence happens at a surprising or satisfying enough point' (Lee 2010: 301). Recurrence in comic texts, therefore, can be said to magnify the humour of gags and other comic structures, bring out the humour in elements not inherently humorous, as well as signal to the receiver that the text is to be perceived as comic.

The relationship between recurrence, dramatic irony and comic surprise/suspense in humorous narratives has been discussed by King (2002: 49) in his account of the 'almost unbearable sense of anticipation' generated in the viewers of those film comedies which construct differential hierarchies of knowledge between the audience and the characters. In order to explain this creation of painful, comic anticipation, he discusses the Warner Bros. Road Runner cartoons to suggest how their 'repeated formula' helps to construct the viewer's knowledge and affect his or her experience of suspense and surprise triggered by story events:

> A similar approach is used in the Warner Bros. Road Runner cartoons, the repeated formula of which assures the viewer that Wile E. Coyote's efforts to catch the Road Runner will *always* fail. About that, there is no surprise; comic suspense and tension is created, however, in the gap between this knowledge and delayed revelation of what *exactly* will go wrong in any particular case.
>
> (King 2002: 49)

This repeated formula which, as King suggests, creates the audience's knowledge of how the story will develop, here will be referred to as recurrence, and will be understood as a repetition of a variant of a particular story event. In what follows, I concentrate on events with humorously negative outcomes, the recurrence of which invites an expectation – or perhaps conviction – of another similarly unsuccessful result. This conviction, importantly, is exclusive to the reader, as the characters involved are blissfully unaware of the disaster which they are heading towards (like the coyote in the Road Runner cartoons). The following examples illustrate how this kind of dramatic irony is created by Jerome K. Jerome, whose use of repetition of a particular type of story event and the speech and thought representation techniques used to describe it add to the creation of comic suspense. In *Three Men in a Boat*, one of the humorously disastrous recurring events is that of cooking, the first instance of which appears when Jerome, the first-person narrator, describes what happened when another character, Harris, decided to make scrambled eggs on their boat:

> **Example 36 (a)**
>
> Harris proposed that we should have scrambled eggs for breakfast. He said he would cook them. It seemed, from his account, that he was very good at doing scrambled eggs. He often did them at picnics and when out on yachts. He was quite famous for them. People who had once tasted his scrambled eggs, so we gathered from his conversation, never cared for any other food afterwards, but pined away and died when they could not get them.
>
> It made our mouths water to hear him talk about the things, and we handed him out the stove and the frying-pan and all the eggs that had not smashed and gone over everything in the hamper, and begged him to begin.
>
> (Jerome [1889] 1993: 103)

This passage not only guides the reader's anticipation as to how the episode will progress, but also gives indication of what the characters' expectations are. Our dubious attitude towards Harris' eggs-cooking skills is cued by the way his words are reported by the first-person narrator Jerome, particularly by the use of *Free Indirect Speech* (*FIS*) which here forms a blend of the speaker's words and the narrator's thoughts. The indirect speech used in the first few sentences ('Harris proposed that ...', 'He said ...') soon gives way to FIS, which blurs the boundary between what was actually said by Harris and what was made up by Jerome. The suggestion that Harris insisted that people who tasted his scrambled eggs 'never cared for any other food afterwards, but pined away and died when they could not get them' may strike the reader as particularly far-fetched, especially when Jerome precedes it with a hedge 'so we gathered from his conversation' which indicates that the actual words were never uttered, but rather that the narrator provides a summary. This use of hyperbolical expressions to report Harris' speech (especially the reference to diners 'pining away and dying') may suggest that the narrator was trying to communicate an air of boastfulness that he noticed when Harris was describing his cooking abilities. It seems, in fact, as if Jerome aims to alert his audience to the fact that Harris is overestimating his talents, and that the whole endeavour will end in failure. The way he recounts Harris' speech communicates what Leech and Short (2007: 262) define as an attitude of *ironic distance* on the part of the narrator, which in this case creates a gap between the different expectations that Harris and the reader have about the progression of the story – a prerequisite to dramatic irony.

A factor which complicates the above interpretation of the passage is that, as it turns out, the first-person narrator Jerome does not actually anticipate that the cooking event will end in failure. On the contrary, he and George immediately hand over the necessary utensils and 'beg' Harris to begin. The only participant in this situation who expects events to spin out of control, it appears, is the reader. How is it possible, then, that Jerome managed to cue us to anticipate disaster, while himself remaining oblivious to impending failure? It seems that Jerome-narrator is in fact a combination of two separate entities: Jerome-character and Jerome-author. It was Jerome-author who was creating the ironic distance between the reader and Harris – and between the reader and Jerome-character, who, as it turns out, is also unable to foresee upcoming story outcomes. This act of secret communion of the author and reader behind the narrator's back (Booth 1961: 300) is an effect of what Booth defines as *unreliable narration*. In humorous fiction, unreliable narration is often associated with narcissistic 'misfit' protagonists (as outlined in the previous chapter). Jerome's misfit qualities and his resulting unreliability as a narrator, to some extent, stop him from making correct assumptions about the development of story events – in that way, he is similar to Bertie Wooster, whose self-involvement prevented him from noticing the signs which indicated forthcoming trouble in the match-making episode.

As anticipated by the reader, the scrambled eggs are not a success – 'all that came out,' recounts Jerome, 'was a teaspoon of burnt and unappetizing-looking mess' (Jerome [1889] 1993: 104). While the dramatic irony in the cooking-themed extract was originally created by unreliable narration and speech representation techniques, the following passage shows how even in the absence of such devices, a subsequent mention of cooking can guide the reader's expectations as to how the story will develop. The extract, in which the characters decide to make an Irish stew, is an example of recurrence, as it is structured as a variant of the scrambled eggs event.

Example 36 (b)
It was still early when we got settled, and George said that, as we had plenty of time, it would be a splendid opportunity to try a good slap-up supper. He said he would show us what could be done up the river in the way of cooking, and suggested that, with the vegetables and the remains of the cold beef and general odds and ends, we should make an Irish stew.
It seemed a fascinating idea. [...]

(Jerome [1889] 1993: 134)

In the light of the previous cooking endeavour in *Three Men in a Boat*, 'It seemed a fascinating idea' is an ominous statement – a cue that trouble is ahead. The choice of words adds to that effect: the modality marker 'seemed' conveys a certain hesitancy which introduces an element of doubt to the meaning of the pre-modifier 'fascinating', signalling its potential negative connotations in the phrase 'a fascinating idea'.

The slightly threatening sense of 'fascinating' will be evident to the reader familiar with the previous occurrence of cooking in the novel, especially since the characters' intention to cook was presented in a similar way – the sentence 'It seemed, from his account, that he was very good at doing scrambled eggs.' from 36 (a), for example, contrasts the hesitant verb 'seemed' with the positive adjective 'very good' in the same way in which it is done in 36 (b). Another cue which can alert the reader that something may go wrong is the slightly patronizing ring to 'He said he would show us what could be done up the river in the way of cooking', which can remind the reader about the previous occurrence in which someone's inflated view of their cooking skills led to disaster.

Apart from signalling impending problems, the sentence 'It seemed a fascinating idea.' communicates something else about the situation – despite the previous cooking-related misfortune, the protagonist fails to draw an analogy between the two and therefore has no idea what is about to happen. The reader, who suspects that the event is going to end in failure, experiences suspense on behalf of the characters, waiting to find out how exactly this failure will occur. Comic suspense lies in a combination of this potentially uncomfortable anticipation of a disaster and a more positive expectation to be amused by the surprising detail of the disaster which the author is keeping from us. Jerome-author does not disappoint – while readers have been prepared for the negative outcome of making the Irish stew, they could not have anticipated how badly it would go. 'Half a pork pie', 'half a tin of potted salmon' and 'a couple of eggs' (Jerome [1889] 1993: 135) are just a few of the unexpected ingredients that end up in the stew, but the surprise culminates when an appearance of the characters' dog with a dead water-rat in its mouth leads to 'a discussion as to whether the rat should go in or not' (Jerome [1889] 1993: 136). While much of the suspense and dramatic irony is provided by recurrence, the humour lies in the writer's ability to strategically list the unexpected stew ingredients so as to evoke comic surprise which leads to amusement. One of the readers of *Three Men in a Boat* describes this experience of suspense and surprise as a response to plot events as:

> [...] you could feel the wrap-up coming, and you knew it would be a surprise.

The use of recurrence is one of the techniques which, by providing readers with clues as to how the story events are likely to progress, allows them to 'feel the wrap-up coming'. The feeling which accompanies waiting for a narrative resolution (or 'wrap-up', as the reader above calls it) is associated with suspense. Suspenseful story structures are constructed so that even though the reader feels that the outcome of a story event is about to be revealed, the knowledge about what exactly that outcome will be is limited. In the case of comic narratives like *Three Men in a Boat*, the only thing we know for certain is that it will be a surprise.

5.4. Conclusion

A typical comic plot is one which involves exposition techniques that prepare the reader for the occurrence of complications which ultimately lead to a happy ending. The amusing potential of humorous complications lies in the comic surprise they trigger and the humorous resolution they lead to once the reader is able to distance him- or herself from the seriousness of the problematic event. While the creation of structures based on surprise is a technique used to evoke amusement and therefore stabilize our experience of comedy, those story structures which rely on our emotional investment in the plot have a different effect. Comic suspense – a complex humorous response which combines tension and amusement – is based on a delayed revelation of a predictable outcome. In comic narratives, it is often created by constructing hierarchies of knowledge in which readers, characters and narrators are provided with varying degrees of information regarding how the story events will develop. The two techniques which allow for such hierarchies of knowledge to be created are dramatic irony (which provides the reader more information about the plot than the characters have) and recurrence (established through repetition of similar story events).

6

Conclusion

This book has explored the relationship between the language of written comic narratives and the emotional responses which may be evoked in the process of reading them. My aim has been to investigate the stylistic elements which shape the affective side of comic narrative comprehension, focusing specifically on the creation and experience of the moods, characters and events which constitute the narrative worlds of comedy. The key to my approach has been the investigation of the full experience of the worlds of comic novels and short stories, meaning that rather than focusing strictly on those texts' potential to amuse, I have also considered the ways in which humour can be made to coexist with other, non-humorous experiential features of narrative comprehension. At the heart of this study, therefore, lies the appreciation that the language of narrative texts allows readers to integrate amusement and other, often negative, emotions.

6.1. Summary

Our emotional experience of reading comic novels and short stories is shaped by a range of stylistic cues, that is, those elements of the linguistic layer of the narrative which signal and elicit emotional responses. While many of the cues found in comic narratives are associated with evoking the positive affective state of amusement, these texts also contain cues which have the potential to trigger more negative emotional responses. Humorous worlds (the narrative worlds of comedy) were therefore said to contain two types of stylistic cue, depending on whether they contribute to our perception of the world as a humorous one or, on the contrary, they trigger responses unrelated to humour. Those cues were referred to as stabilizing and destabilizing cues, and they were classified according to whether they stabilize our experience of humour, or destabilize it by triggering non-humorous emotion. Stabilizing and destabilizing cues can occur independently and lead to either amusement or a non-humorous, negative emotion. The experience of a humorous world, however, was said to be based partly on what I called a complex humorous response, which is a blend of amusement and a negative emotion. Complex humorous responses, I argued, are evoked when the two types of cue – stabilizing and destabilizing cues – are presented simultaneously. The three central chapters of this book have explored the various stabilizing and destabilizing cues found in comic novels and short stories, suggesting how writers use language to trigger moods, manipulate representations of people and construct event trajectories which affect our experience of humorous narrative worlds in different ways.

Chapter 3 (Experiencing modes and moods) explored some of the techniques which allow writers to evoke cognitive and affective predispositions towards experiencing amusement in their readers. Those comic predispositions, a humorous mode (a cognitive expectation of humour) and a humorous mood (an affective expectation of amusement), can be stabilized by the use of paratexts which frame the text as a comedy, intrinsically humorous lines which evoke amusement, as well the distancing and downgrading techniques which encourage a detached perspective and a mocking attitude. These humorous predispositions, however, can be temporarily destabilized by the negative emotional charge of what are referred to as dark elements, the appearance of which can lead to such effects as mood shifts, dark humour and blends of humorous and non-humorous moods.

Following from the discussion of moods, Chapter 4 (Engaging with characters) explored the uses and potential effects of characterization in comic narratives. Character humour creation, I argued, relies on manipulations of social stereotypes and the use of humorous stock types. One of those types is the eccentric, disruptive misfit, who becomes a source of humour particularly when placed in interactions with other characters, leading him or her to cause miscommunication and express impoliteness. While the above characterization techniques were considered stabilizing cues, destabilizing comedy was linked to constructing another character type, the sympathetic everyman/everywoman. It is this type who, when placed in awkward social situations, may elicit complex humorous responses based on combinations of amusement and painful self-reflective emotions such as the embarrassment or shame experienced through cringe humour.

Chapter 5 (Reacting to story structures), finally, moved from the consideration of comic characters to the investigation of the situations which happen to them. Specifically, it focused on the techniques which manipulate the presentation of story events in narrative comedy. A typical plot trajectory of a comic narrative is one which features comic foreshadowing that prepares the reader for the occurrence of humorous complications, and which concludes in a happy ending. While the emotion of surprise as a response to amusing story events was said to stabilize the experience of comedy, it was contrasted with the feeling of suspense, which destabilizes that experience by introducing a non-humorous state of tense anticipation. Comic suspense, therefore, can be viewed as an experiential feature of comic narratives, based on a blend of amusement and a more uncomfortable, negative feeling.

The two aspects of stabilizing and destabilizing the experience of humorous worlds which have been referred to at various stages throughout this work are distance and immersion. That is because my approach to the intersection of language and emotion in comic narratives was based on the dichotomy between those stylistic features which provide the distance necessary to perceive the world-based entities as amusing, and those which suspend that humorousness by inviting readers to immerse themselves in the narrative world and become vulnerable to the 'serious' emotions incompatible with humour.

Table 2 Cues, techniques and effects

NARRATIVE WORLD COMPONENT	QUALITY	CUE	TECHNIQUE	EFFECT
Moods	Stabilizing	Paratext	Shaping expectations through cover design, title, prologue	Humorous mode/mood
		Inherently amusing line	Using incongruity to create humorous one-liners	
		Distancing	Drawing attention to the stylistic layer of the text or to the act of storytelling	
		Downgrading	Deprecating or downplaying textual entities	
	Destabilizing	'Dark' (negatively charged) element	Introduction of a dark element using a buffer	Mood switch
			Juxtaposing a dark element with a humorous one	Dark humour
			Exaggerating a dark element to the point of unrealistic	
			Presenting a non-serious element as excessively dark	
			Downplaying/distancing a dark element while cueing immersion in narrative world	Mood blend

Characters	Stabilizing	Manipulated stereotype	Exaggerating an easily accessible stereotype	Laughing at a character
		'Misfit' stock type	Combining features of impostor, buffoon and churl Presenting a character to stand out	
		Misfit character creates social disruption	A misfit character behaves in a socially inappropriate way	
		Miscommunication	Characters talk at cross-purposes	
		Impoliteness	A character is being verbally aggressive	
	Destabilizing	'Every(wo)man' protagonist	Constructing autobiographical alignment	Identification with a character
			Constructing a prototype of an inclusive social category	
			Creating an impression of closeness/proximity to character	Illusion of intimacy with a character
			Adding self-deprecation to character's speech and thought	Liking for a character
	'Every(wo)man'/'misfit' protagonist blend	Mock narcissism in a reliable every(wo)man protagonist	Laughing with a character
			Narcissistic qualities in an unreliable every(wo)man protagonist	
			Exaggerated narcissism and exaggerated self-deprecation in an every(wo)man/misfit blend	
		Every(wo)man protagonist causes social disruption	Every(wo)man protagonist behaves in a socially inappropriate way	Cringe humour
			Free Indirect Discourse simultaneously cues empathy and distance	

(Continued)

Table 2 (Continued)

NARRATIVE WORLD COMPONENT	QUALITY	CUE	TECHNIQUE	EFFECT
Story structures	Stabilizing	Comic foreshadowing	Scattering of preview statements in the opening	Anticipation of a comic plot trajectory
		Humorous complication	Building a problematic event with unexpected or incongruous qualities	Comic surprise
			Using distancing techniques to present a problematic event as not serious	Humorous resolution
			Structuring an event to lead to a swift humorous resolution	
		Happy ending	Ending a narrative by restoring the desired status quo	Comic plot resolution
	Destabilizing	Suspenseful humorous complication	Structuring an event around predictability of a particular course of events and delay in revealing how exactly the events develop	Comic suspense
		Dramatic irony	Speech and thought representation strategies which create a gap between readers' and characters' level of knowledge about plot events	
			Recurrence of similar events with humorously negative outcomes	

6.2. Concluding remarks

Comic novels and short stories are stylistically constructed not only to evoke the response of amusement which is typically associated with humour, but also to trigger a range of other, non-humorous emotions which add to our experience of comic texts. The right balance in mixing the humorous and non-humorous elements which coexist in comedy, as one reader of Joseph Heller's *Catch-22* points out, lies at the heart of the pleasure of reading comic narratives:

> Never have I been pulled through the entire spectrum of emotion quite as enjoyably as this, with Heller ingeniously switching tones on a dime with a magician's charm. One moment I was laughing like a fool, and the next I was clenching my jaw with agony at the horrors of the war; thankfully for my taste, Heller leaned more on the comedic/optimistic side.

The combination of conflicting emotional states triggered by the novel – described by the reader as 'switching tones on a dime' – underlies the approach to the experience of comic narratives developed in this book. Here, these complex, multifaceted experiential features of narrative comedy have been examined stylistically, that is, discussed in relation to the various textual cues which give rise to them. Such an exploration of the language of comic narratives, when complemented by an investigation of the affective aspects of comic narrative comprehension, provides key observations not only about comedy's ability to pull us through 'the entire spectrum of emotion' in the course of reading, but also about the sources of gratification which narrative comedy offers its readers. Rather than existing purely for the purpose of amusing their readers, comic novels and short stories offer a wide range of affective returns, allowing us to enjoy the experience of painful or negative emotions by placing them in the safe context of a humorous narrative world.

Notes

Chapter 1

1 Goodreads reviews will be used throughout to discuss readers' reactions to the texts analysed here, as explained in more detail further in this chapter (1.3.).

Chapter 4

1 The 'misfit' humorous stock type label, in a way in which it is used in this book, has been informed by the documentary series *The United States of Television: America in Primetime* (BBC, 2013), which is devoted to the most influential characters in American television programmes.

References

Abrams, M. H. and G. Harpman (2012), *A Glossary of Literary Terms*, 10th edn, Boston: Wadsworth.

Adams, D. ([1979] 2002), *The Hitchhiker's Guide to the Galaxy*, London: Picador.

Allbritton, D. W. and R. J. Gerrig (1991), 'Participatory Responses in Text Understanding', *Journal of Memory and Language*, 30: 603–26.

Apter, M. J. (1982), *The Experience of Motivation: The Theory of Psychological Motivation*, London, New York: Academic Press.

Apter, M. J. (1991), 'A Structural Phenomenology of Play', in J. H. Kerr and M. J. Apter (eds), *Adult Play: A Reversal Theory Approach*, 13–29, Amsterdam: Swets and Zeitlinger.

Arnold, M. B. (1961), *Emotion and Personality*, vol. 1, London: Cassell.

Attardo, S. (1998), 'The Analysis of Humorous Narratives', *HUMOR*, 11 (3): 231–60.

Attardo, S. (2001), *Humorous Texts: A Semantic and Pragmatic Analysis*, Berlin, New York: Mouton de Gruyter.

Attardo, S. (2002), 'Cognitive Stylistics of Humorous Texts', in E. Semino and J. Culpeper (eds), *Cognitive Stylistics: Language and Cognition in Text Analysis*, 231–50, Amsterdam, Philadelphia: John Benjamins.

Attardo, S. and V. Raskin (1991), 'Script Theory Revis(it)ed: Joke Similarity and Joke Representation Model', *HUMOR*, 4 (3–4): 293–347.

Baldick, C. (2008), *The Oxford Dictionary of Literary Terms*, 3rd edn, Oxford: Oxford University Press.

Baron-Cohen, S. (1995), *Mindblindness: An Essay on Autism and Theory of Mind*, Cambridge, MA; London: MIT Press.

Bartlett, F. C. ([1932] 1995), *Remembering: A Study in Experimental and Social Psychology*, Cambridge: Cambridge University Press.

Bateson, G. ([1972] 2006), 'A Theory of Play and Fantasy', in K. Salen and E. Zimmerman (eds), *The Game Design Reader: A Rules of Play Anthology*, 314–28, Cambridge, MA; London: The MIT Press.

Bergson, H. (1913), *Laughter: An Essay on the Meaning of the Comic*, London: Macmillan and Co., Limited.

Berlyne, D. E. (1972), 'Humor and Its Kin', in J. H. Goldstein and P. E. McGhee (eds), *The Psychology of Humour: Theoretical Perspectives and Empirical Issues*, 43–59, New York, London: Academic Press.

Billig, M. (2005), *Laughter and Ridicule: Towards a Social Critique of Humour*, London: SAGE.

Bloom, H. (ed.), (2010), *Dark Humor*, New York: Bloom's Literary Criticism.

Booth, W. C. (1961), *The Rhetoric of Fiction*, Chicago: University of Chicago Press.

Bousfield, D. (2008), *Impoliteness in Interaction*, Amsterdam, Philadelphia: John Benjamins.

Bowlby, J. ([1969] 1997), *Attachment and Loss*, vol. 1, London: Pimlico.

Bray, J. (2007), 'The Effects of Free Indirect Discourse: Empathy Revisited', in M. Lambrou and P. Stockwell (eds), *Contemporary Stylistics*, 56–67, London, New York: Continuum.

Brewer, W. F. (1996), 'The Nature of Narrative Suspense and the Problem of Rereading', in P. Vorderer, H. J. Wulff and M. Friedrichsen (eds), *Suspense: Conceptualizations, Theoretical Analyses, and Empirical Explorations*, 107–27, London, New York: Routledge.

Brewer, W. F. and E. H. Lichtenstein (1982), 'Stories Are to Entertain: A Structural-affect Theory of Stories', *Journal of Pragmatics*, 6: 473–86.

Bridget Jones's Diary (2001), [Film] Dir. Sharon Maguire, UK: United International Pictures.

Brown, P. and S. C. Levinson (1987), *Politeness: Some Universals in Language Use*, Cambridge: Cambridge University Press.

Cantor, J. R., J. Bryant and D. Zillmann (1974), 'Enhancement of Humor Appreciation by Transferred Excitation', *Journal of Personality and Social Psychology*, 30 (6): 812–21.

Chatman, S. (1978), *Story and Discourse: Narrative Structure in Fiction and Film*, Ithaca, London: Cornell University Press.

Chory, R. M. (2010), 'Media Entertainment and Verbal Aggression: Contents, Effects, and Correlates', in T. A. Avtgis and A. S. Rancer (eds), *Arguments, Aggression, and Conflict: New Directions in Theory and Research*, 176–97, London: Routledge.

Cohen, J. (2004), 'Parasocial Break-up from Favorite Television Characters: The Role of Attachment Styles and Relationship Intensity', *Journal of Social and Personal Relationships*, 21 (2): 187–202.

Cohen, J. (2006), 'Audience Identification with Media Characters', in J. Bryant and P. Vorderer (eds), *Psychology of Entertainment*, 183–97, Mahwah, NJ: Lawrence Erlbaum.

Conway, M. A. and D. A. Bekerian (1987), 'Situational Knowledge and Emotions', *Cognition and Emotion*, 1 (2): 145–91.

Cox, C. (2011), 'Catch-22: 50 Years Later', *The Guardian*, 10 October. Available online: http://www.theguardian.com/books/2011/oct/10/catch-22-50-years-joseph-heller (accessed 23 January 2015).

Culpeper, J. (1996), 'Towards an Anatomy of Impoliteness', *Journal of Pragmatics*, 25: 349–67.

Culpeper, J. (2000), 'A Cognitive Approach to Characterization: Katherina in Shakespeare's *The Taming of the Shrew*', *Language and Literature*, 9 (4): 291–316.

Culpeper, J. (2001), *Language and Characterisation: People in Plays and Other Texts*, Harlow: Pearson.

Culpeper, J. (2011), *Impoliteness: Using Language to Cause Offence*, Cambridge: Cambridge University Press.

Dancygier, B. (2011), *The Language of Stories: A Cognitive Approach*, Cambridge: Cambridge University Press.

Davies, C. (1998), *Jokes and Their Relation to Society*, Berlin, New York: Mouton de Gruyter.

Davis, M. H. (1994), *Empathy: A Social Psychological Approach*, Madison, Dubuque: Brown and Benchmark.

Doležel, L. (1989), 'Possible Worlds and Literary Fictions', in S. Allén (ed.), *Possible Worlds in Humanities, Arts and Sciences: Proceedings of Nobel Symposium 65*, 221–42, Berlin, New York: Mouton de Gruyter.

Double, O. (1997), *Stand-Up! On Being a Comedian*, London: Methuen.

Douglas, M. (1968), 'The Social Control of Cognition: Some Factors in Joke Perception', *Man*, 3: 361–76.

Dynel, M. (2011), 'Joker in the Pack: Towards Determining the Status of Humorous Framing in Conversations', in M. Dynel (ed.), *The Pragmatics of Humour across Discourse Domains*, 217–41, Amsterdam, Philadelphia: John Benjamins.

Dynel, M. (2013), 'Impoliteness as Disaffiliative Humour in Film Talk', in M. Dynel (ed.), *Developments in Linguistic Humour Theory*, 105–44, Amsterdam, Philadelphia: John Benjamins.

Emmott, C. (1994), 'Frames of Reference: Contextual Monitoring and Narrative Discourse', in M. R. Coulthard (ed.), *Advances in Written Text Analysis*, 157–66, London: Routledge.

Emmott, C. (1997), *Narrative Comprehension*, Oxford: Oxford University Press.

Emmott, C., M. Alexander and A. Marszalek (2014), 'Schema Theory in Stylistics', in M. Burke (ed.), *The Routledge Handbook of Stylistics*, 268–83, London: Routledge.

Ermida, I. (2008), *The Language of Comic Narratives: Humor Construction in Short Stories*, Berlin, New York: Mouton de Gruyter.
Ermida, I. (2009), 'Guilty Laughter: On the Ethics of Humour', *Diacrítica, Filosofia e Cultura*, 23 (2): 361–3.
Ferguson, M. A. and T. E. Ford (2008), 'Disparagement Humor: A Theoretical and Empirical Review of Psychoanalytic, Superiority, and Social Identity Theories', *HUMOR*, 21 (3): 283–312.
Fielding, H. ([1996] 1998), *Bridget Jones's Diary*, London: Picador.
Forabosco, G. (2008), 'Is the Concept of Incongruity Still a Useful Construct for the Advancement of Humor Research?', *Lodz Papers in Pragmatics*, 4.1, Special Issue on Humour: 45–62.
Forster, E. M. (1962 [1927]), *Aspects of the Novel*, London: Penguin.
Four Weddings and a Funeral (1994), [Film] Dir. Mike Newell, UK: Rank Film Distributors.
Freud, S. ([1905] 1960), *Jokes and Their Relation to the Unconscious*, ed. and trans. J. Strachey, New York, London: W.W. Norton & Company.
Friedman, B. J. (1969), *Black Humor*, New York: Bentam.
Frijda, N. (1986), *The Emotions*, Cambridge: Cambridge University Press.
Frijda, N. (2007), *The Laws of Emotion*, Mahwah, NJ: Lawrence Erlbaum Associates.
Frye, N. (1957), *Anatomy of Criticism: Four Essays*, Princeton, NJ: Princeton University Press.
Gavins, J. (2007), *Text World Theory: An Introduction*, Edinburgh: Edinburgh University Press.
Gavins, J. (2013), *Reading the Absurd*, Edinburgh: Edinburgh University Press.
Genette, G. (1980), *Narrative Discourse*, Ithaca, New York: Cornell University Press.
Genette, G. (1997), *Paratexts: Thresholds of Interpretation*, Cambridge: Cambridge University Press.
Gerrig, R. J. (1993), *Experiencing Narrative Worlds: On the Psychological Activities of Reading*, New Haven, London: Yale University Press.
Gibbs, R. W. Jr. (2005), *Embodiment and Cognitive Science*, Cambridge: Cambridge University Press.
Giles, D. C. (2002), 'Parasocial Interaction: A Review of the Literature and a Model for Future Research', *Media Psychology*, 4 (3): 279–305.
Goffman, E. ([1967] 1972), *Interaction Ritual: Essays on Face-to-Face Behavior*, Harmondsworth: Penguin.

Gray, F. (2005), 'Privacy, Embarrassment and Social Power: British Sitcom', in S. Lockyer and M. Pickering (eds), *Beyond a Joke: The Limits of Humour*, 146–61, Basingstoke, New York: Palgrave Macmillan.

Green, M. C. and T. C. Brock (2000), 'The Role of Transportation in the Persuasiveness of Public Narratives', *Journal of Personality and Social Psychology*, 79 (5): 701–21.

Green, M. C. (2010), 'Transportation into Narrative Worlds: The Role of Prior Knowledge and Perceived Realism', *Discourse Processes*, 38 (2): 247–66.

Green, M. C., T. C. Brock and G. F. Kaufman (2004), 'Understanding Media Enjoyment: The Role of Transportation into Narrative Worlds', *Communication Theory*, 14 (4): 311–27.

Greengross, G. and G. Miller (2008), 'Humor Ability Reveals Intelligence, Predicts Mating Success, and is Higher in Males', *Intelligence*, 39 (4): 188–92.

Greenwood, D. N. (2008), 'Television as Escape from Self: Psychological Predictors of Media Involvement', *Personality and Individual Differences*, 44: 414–24.

Grice, H. P. (1975), 'Logic and Conversation', in P. Cole and J. Morgan (eds), *Syntax and Semantics 3: Speech Acts*, 41–58, London, New York: Academic Press.

Haddon, M. (2007), *A Spot of Bother*, London: Vintage.

Hakemulder, J. and E. Koopman (2010), 'Readers Closing in on Immoral Characters' Consciousness. Effects of Free Indirect Discourse on Response to Literary Narratives', *Journal of Literary Theory*, 4 (1): 41–62.

Harvey, W. J. (1966), *Character and the Novel*, London: Chatto and Windus.

Havránek, B. (1964), 'The Functional Differentiation of the Standard Language', in P. L. Garvin (ed.), *The Prague School Reader on Aesthetics, Literary Structure and Style*, 3–16, Washington DC: Georgetown Press.

Heller, J. ([1961] 1994), *Catch-22*, London: Vintage.

Hobbes, T. ([1651] 1996), *Leviathan*, ed. R. Tuck, Cambridge: Cambridge University Press.

Hoey, M. (2001), *Textual Interaction: An Introduction to Written Discourse Analysis*, London: Routledge.

Hornby, N. (1995), *High Fidelity*, London: Penguin.

Horton, D. and R. R. Wohl (1956), 'Mass Communication and Para-social Interaction: Observations of Intimacy at a Distance', *Psychiatry*, 19: 215–29.

In Bruges (2008), [Film] Dir. Martin McDonagh), UK, USA: Universal Studios, Focus Features.

Jerome, J. K. ([1889] 1993), *Three Men in a Boat (To Say Nothing of the Dog!)*, Ware: Wordsworth Editions Limited.
Keen, S. (2006), 'A Theory of Narrative Empathy', *Narrative*, 14 (3): 207–36.
Keen, S. (2007), *Empathy and the Novel*, Oxford: Oxford University Press.
King, G. (2002), *Film Comedy*, London, New York: Wallflower.
King, G. (2011), 'Striking a Balance between Culture and Fun: "Quality" Meets Hitman Genre in *In Bruges*', *New Review of Film and Television Studies*, 9 (2): 132–51.
Kuzmičová, A. (2012), 'Presence in the Reading of Literary Narrative: A Case for Motor Enactment', *Semiotica*, 189 (1/4): 23–48.
La Fave, L. (1972), 'Humor Judgments as a Function of Reference Groups and Identification Classes', in J. H. Goldstein and P. E. McGhee (eds), *The Psychology of Humor: Theoretical Perspectives and Empirical Issues*, 195–210, New York: Academic Press.
Larkin Galiñanes, C. (2000), 'Relevance Theory, Humour and the Narrative Structure of Humorous Novels', *Revista Alicantina Ingleses*, 13: 95–106.
Larkin Galiñanes, C. (2002), 'Narrative Structure in Humorous Novels: The Case of *Lucky Jim*', *Babel A. F. I. A. L.*, Numero extraordinario: 141–70.
Larkin Galiñanes, C. (2010), 'How to Tackle Humour in Literary Narratives', in C. Valero-Garces (ed.), *Dimensions of Humor. Explorations in Linguistics, Literature, Cultural Studies and Translation*, 199–223, Valencia: Servicio de Publicaciones de la Universidad.
Lee, S. (2010), *How I Escaped My Certain Fate: The Life and Deaths of a Stand-Up Comedian*, London: Faber and Faber.
Leech, G. (1983), *Principles of Pragmatics*, London: Longman.
Leech, G. and M. Short (2007), *Style in Fiction. A Linguistic Introduction to English Fictional Prose*, 2nd edn, Harlow: Pearson Education Limited.
Lehnert, W. G. and E. W. Vine (1987), 'The Role of Affect in Narrative Structure', *Cognition and Emotion*, 1 (3): 299–322.
Lewis, M. (2008), 'Self-conscious Emotions: Embarrassment, Pride, Shame, and Guilt', in M. Lewis, J. M. Haviland-Jones and L. Feldman Barrett (eds), *Handbook of Emotions*, 3rd edn, 742–56, New York, London: The Guilford Press.
Lewycka, M. ([2005] 2006), *A Short History of Tractors in Ukrainian*, London: Penguin.
Long, D. L. and A. C. Graesser (1988), 'Wit and Humor in Discourse Processing', *Discourse Processes*, 11 (1): 35–60.

Lundy, D. E., J. Tan and M. R. Cunningham (1998), 'Heterosexual Romantic Preferences: The Importance of Humor and Physical Attractiveness for Different Types of Relationships', *Personal Relationships*, 5 (3): 311–25.

Lyall, S. (2008), 'What You Read Is What He Is, Sort of', *The New York Times*, 8 June. Available online: http://www.nytimes.com/2008/06/08/books/08lyal.html?pagewanted=all&_r=0 (accessed 26 January 2015).

Lynn, J. (2011), *Comedy Rules: From the Cambridge Footlights to Yes Prime Minister*, London: Faber and Faber.

Marszalek, A. (2013), '"It's not funny out of context!": A Cognitive Stylistic Approach to Humorous Narratives', in M. Dynel (ed.), *Developments in Linguistic Humour Theory*, 393–421, Amsterdam, Philadelphia: John Benjamins.

Marszalek, A. (2016a), 'The Humorous Worlds of Film Comedy', in J. Gavins, and E. Lahey (eds), *World Building: Discourse in the Mind*, 203–19, London: Bloomsbury.

Marszalek, A. (2016b), 'Beyond Amusement: Language and Emotion in Narrative Comedy', PhD thesis, University of Glasgow.

Marszalek, A. (2019), 'Constructing Inferiority through Comic Characterisation: Self-deprecating Humour and Cringe Comedy in *High Fidelity* and *Bridget Jones's Diary*', in B. Neurohr and L. Stewart-Shaw (eds), *Experiencing Fictional Worlds: Where Does a Text Take a Reader?*, 119–34, Amsterdam, Philadelphia: John Benjamins.

Martin, R. (2007), *The Psychology of Humor: An Integrative Approach*, London: Elsevier.

Miall, D. S. (1989), 'Beyond the Schema Given: Affective Comprehension of Literary Narratives', *Cognition and Emotion*, 3 (1): 55–78.

Miall, D. S. (1995), 'Anticipation and Feeling in Literary Response: A Neuropsychological Perspective', *Poetics*, 23: 275–98.

Miall, D. S. (2007), *Literary Reading: Empirical and Theoretical Studies*, New York: Peter Lang.

Milligan, S. (1971), *Adolf Hitler: My Part in His Downfall*, London: Michael Joseph Limited.

Montoro, R. (2007), 'Stylistics of Cappuccino Fiction: A Socio-cognitive Perspective', in M. Lambrou and P. Stockwell (eds), *Contemporary Stylistics*, 68–80, London, New York: Continuum.

Morreall, J. (1987a), 'A New Theory of Laughter', in J. Morreall (ed.), *The Philosophy of Laughter and Humor*, 128–38, New York: State University of New York Press.

Morreall, J. (1987b), 'Funny Ha-ha, Funny Strange, and Other Reactions to Incongruity', in J. Morreall (ed.), *The Philosophy of Laughter and Humor*, 188–207, New York: State University of New York Press.

Morreall, J. (2009), *Comic Relief: A Comprehensive Philosophy of Humor*, Chichester: Wiley-Blackwell.

Mukařovský, J. (1964), 'Standard Language and Poetic Language', in P. L. Garvin (ed.), *The Prague School Reader on Aesthetics, Literary Structure and Style*, 17–30, Washington, DC: Georgetown Press.

Mulkay, M. (1988), *On Humour. Its Nature and Its Place in Modern Society*, Cambridge: Polity Press.

Murgatroyd, S. (1985), 'Introduction to Reversal Theory', in M. J. Apter, D. Fontana and S. Murgatroyd (eds), *Reversal Theory: Applications and Developments*, 1–19, Cardiff: University College Cardiff Press.

Nash, W. (1985), *The Language of Humour: Style and Technique in Comic Discourse*, New York: Longman.

Neale, S. and F. Krutnik (1990), *Popular Film and Television Comedy*, London, New York: Routledge.

Nell, V. (1988), 'The Psychology of Reading for Pleasure: Needs and Gratifications', *Reading Research Quarterly*, 23 (1): 6–50.

Oatley, K. (1994), 'A Taxonomy of the Emotions of Literary Response and a Theory of Identification in Fictional Narrative', *Poetics*, 23: 53–74.

Oatley, K. (2011), *Such Stuff as Dreams: The Psychology of Fiction*, Chichester: Wiley-Blackwell.

Obrdlik, A. J. (1942), '"Gallows Humor" – A Sociological Phenomenon', *American Journal of Sociology*, 47 (5): 709–16.

Palmer, J. (1994), *Taking Humour Seriously*, London, New York: Routledge.

Parkinson, B. (1995), *Ideas and Realities of Emotion*, London: Routledge.

Parkinson, B., P. Totterdell, R. B. Briner and S. Reynolds (1996), *Changing Moods: The Psychology of Mood and Mood Regulation*, London, New York: Longman.

Pavel, T. G. (1986), *Fictional Worlds*, Cambridge, MA; London: Harvard University Press.

Peplow, D. and R. Carter (2014), 'Stylistics and Real Readers', in M. Burke (ed.), *The Routledge Handbook of Stylistics*, 440–54, London, New York: Routledge.

Peplow, D., J. Swann, P. Trimarco and S. Whiteley (2015), *The Discourse of Reading Groups: Integrating Cognitive and Sociocultural Perspectives*, New York: Routledge.

Propp, V. ([1968] 1975), *Morphology of the Folktale*, 2nd edn, trans. L. Scott, Austin: University of Texas Press.

Raney, A. A. (2004), 'Expanding Disposition Theory: Reconsidering Character Liking, Moral Evaluations, and Enjoyment', *Communication Theory*, 14 (4): 348–69.

Raney, A. A. (2006), 'The Psychology of Disposition-based Theories of Media Enjoyment', in J. Bryant and P. Vorderer (eds), *Psychology of Entertainment*, 137–50, Mahwah, NJ: Lawrence Erlbaum.

Raskin, V. (1985), *Semantic Mechanisms of Humor*, Dordrecht: Reidel.

Rumelhart, D. E. (1980), 'Schemata: The Building Blocks of Cognition', in R. J. Spiro, B. C. Bruce and W. F. Brewer (eds), *Theoretical Issues in Reading Comprehension: Perspectives from Cognitive Psychology, Linguistics, Artificial Intelligence and Education*, 33–58, Hillsdale, NJ: Lawrence Erlbaum.

Russell, J. A. (1980), 'A Circumplex Model of Affect', *Journal of Personality and Social Psychology*, 39: 1161–78.

Ryan, M.-L. (1980), 'Fiction, Non-factuals, and the Principle of Minimal Departure', *Poetics*, 9: 403–22.

Ryan, M.-L. (1991), *Possible Worlds, Artificial Intelligence, and Narrative Theory*, Bloomington, IN: Indiana University Press.

Sanford, A. J. and C. Emmott (2012), *Mind, Brain and Narrative*, Cambridge: Cambridge University Press.

Schopenhauer, A. ([1819] 1969), *The World as Will and Representation*, vol. 1, trans. E. F. J. Payne, New York: Dover Publications.

Sedaris, D. ([2000] 2002), *Me Talk Pretty One Day*, London: Abacus.

Semino, E. (1997), *Language and World Creation in Poems and Other Texts*, London: Longman.

Shklovsky, V. B. ([1917] 1965), 'Art as Technique', in L. T. Lemon and M. J. Reis (eds), *Russian Formalist Criticism: Four Essays*, 3–24, Lincoln: University of Nebraska Press.

Simpson, P. (2006), 'Humor: Stylistic Approaches', in K. Brown (ed.), *Encyclopedia of Language and Linguistics*, 2nd edn, 426–29, London: Elsevier.

Simpson, P. (2011), '"That's Not Ironic, That's Just Stupid": Toward an Eclectic Account of the Discourse of Irony', in M. Dynel (ed.), *The Pragmatics of Humour across Discourse Domains*, 33–50, Amsterdam, Philadelphia: John Benjamins.

Smith, G. M. (2003), *Film Structure and the Emotion System*, Cambridge: Cambridge University Press.

Smith, S. (2000), *Hitchcock: Suspense, Humour and Tone*, London: British Film Institute.

Spencer, H. (1860), 'On the Physiology of Laughter'. Available online: http://www.gutenberg.org/files/16510/16510-h/16510-h.htm#page_298 (accessed 26 May 2015).

Sternberg, M. (1978), *Expositional Modes and Temporal Ordering in Fiction*, Baltimore: Johns Hopkins University Press.

Stivers, R. (2000), *Hair of the Dog: Irish Drinking and Its American Stereotype*, London: Continuum.

Stockwell, P. (2009), *Texture: A Cognitive Aesthetics of Reading*, Edinburgh: Edinburgh University Press.

Stockwell, P. (2014), 'Atmosphere and Tone', in P. Stockwell and S. Whiteley (eds), *The Cambridge Handbook of Stylistics*, 360–74, Cambridge: Cambridge University Press.

Suls, J. M. (1972), 'A Two-stage Model for the Appreciation of Jokes and Cartoons: An Information-processing Analysis', in J. H. Goldstein and P. E. McGhee (eds), *The Psychology of Humour. Theoretical Perspectives and Empirical Issues*, 81–99, New York, London: Academic Press.

Swann, J. and D. Allington (2009), 'Reading Groups and the Language of Literary Texts: A Case Study in Social Reading', *Language and Literature*, 18 (3): 247–64.

Tan, E. S.-H. (1994), 'Film-induced Affect and Witness Emotion', *Poetics*, 23: 7–32.

Tan, E. S.-H. (1995), *Emotion and the Structure of Narrative Film: Film as an Emotion Machine*, Mahwah, NJ: Lawrence Erlbaum.

The United States of Television: America in Primetime (2013), [TV programme] BBC 2, 25 September.

Tobin, V. (2009), 'Cognitive Bias and the Poetics of Surprise', *Language and Literature*, 18 (2): 155–72.

Townsend, S. ([1982] 2002), *The Secret Diary of Adrian Mole, Aged 13¾*, London: Puffin.

Triezenberg, K. E. (2004), 'Humor Enhancers in the Study of Humorous Literature', *HUMOR*, 17 (4): 411–18.

Triezenberg, K. E. (2008), 'Humor in Literature', in V. Raskin (ed.), *The Primer of Humor Research*, 523–42, Berlin, New York: Mouton de Gruyter.

Tsur, R. (1989), 'Horror Jokes, Black Humor, and Cognitive Poetics', *HUMOR*, 2 (3): 243–55.

van Dijk, T. A. (1975), 'Action, Action Description, and Narrative', *New Literary History*, 6 (2): 273–94.
van Dijk, T. A. (1989), 'Structures and Strategies of Discourse and Prejudice', in J. P. van Oudenhoven and T. M. Willemsen (eds), *Ethnic Minorities: Social Psychological Perspectives*, 115–38, Amsterdam: Swets and Zeitlinger.
van Peer, W. (1986), *Stylistics and Psychology: Investigations of Foregrounding*, London, Sydney, Wolfeboro: Croom Helm.
van Peer, W. and J. Hakemulder (2006), 'Foregrounding', in K. Brown (ed.), *Encyclopedia of Language and Linguistics*, 2nd edn, 546–51, Oxford: Elsevier.
Vandelanotte, L. (2010), 'Where am I, Lurking in What Place of Vantage? The Discourse of Distance in John Banville's Fiction', *English Text Construction*, 3 (2): 203–25.
Vermeule, B. (2010), *Why Do We Care about Literary Characters?*, Baltimore: Johns Hopkins University Press.
Wales, K. (2011), *A Dictionary of Stylistics*, 3rd edn, Harlow: Pearson Education Limited.
Watson, D. and A. Tellegen (1985), 'Toward a Consensual Structure of Mood', *Psychological Bulletin*, 98: 219–35.
Werth, P. (1999), *Text Worlds: Representing Conceptual Space in Discourse*, Harlow: Longman.
Wodehouse, P. G. ([1934] 2008), *Right Ho, Jeeves*, London: Arrow Books.
Wolff, H. A., C. E. Smith and H. A. Murray (1934), 'The Psychology of Humor', *The Journal of Abnormal and Social Psychology*, 28 (4): 341–65.
Woodward, S. (2010), 'Curbing Our Enthusiasm: The Cringe Comedy of Sacha Baron Cohen, Ricky Gervais, and Larry David', *Paper at Tea and Talk series*, Bishop's University, Lennoxville, Quebec.
Wright, B. (2011), '"Why Would You Do That, Larry?": Identity Formation and Humor in *Curb Your Enthusiasm*', *The Journal of Popular Culture*, 44 (3): 661–77.
Zillmann, D. (1983), 'Disparagement Humor', in P. E. McGhee and J. H. Goldstein (eds), *Handbook of Humor Research*, vol. 1, 85–107, New York: Springer.
Zillmann, D. (1991), 'Empathy: Affect Bearing Witness to the Emotion of Others', in J. Bryant and D. Zillmann (eds), *Responding to the Screen: Reception and Reaction Processes*, 133–63, Hillsdale, NJ: Lawrence Erlbaum.

Zillmann, D. (2006), 'Empathy: Affective Reactivity to Others' Emotional Experiences', in J. Bryant and P. Vorderer (eds), *Psychology of Entertainment*, 151–81, Mahwah, NJ: Lawrence Erlbaum.

Zillman, D. and H. S. Stocking (1976), 'Putdown Humor', *Journal of Communication*, 26: 154–63.

Zillmann, D. and J. R. Cantor ([1976] 1996), 'A Disposition Theory of Humour and Mirth', in A. J. Chapman and H. C. Foot (eds), *Humour and Laughter: Theory, Research and Applications*, 2nd edn, 93–116, New Brunswick, London: Transaction Publishers.

Zillmann, D. and J. R. Cantor (1977), 'Affective Responses to the Emotions of a Protagonist', *Journal of Experimental Social Psychology*, 13: 155–65.

Zunshine, L. (2006), *Why We Read Fiction: Theory of Mind and the Novel*, Columbus: The Ohio State University Press.

Index

absurd humour   21, 67–8
accommodation, of personality   89, 100
Adams, D.   64, 128
Adolf Hitler: My Part in His Downfall (Milligan)   37, 40, 55
affective disposition   74, 90
affective expectation   35
affective states   28, 33, 34, 42, 47, 145
affective tone   28
agroikos (churl)   76, 77
alazon (imposter)   76, 77
Allbritton, D. W.   11, 114, 126
ambience   30, 62
Amis, K.   24
amusement and humour, link between   7
Apter, M. J.   45
articulated gags   119, 120
atmosphere   29, 30
attachment theory   92
Attardo, S.   22, 23, 116, 137
attitude schemata   50, 72
attitudinal positioning   24
authorial tone   29
autobiographical alignment   88

Banter Principle   84
Bartlett, F. C.   50
Bateson, G.   32
Bergson, H.   20, 47
Berlyne, D. E.   21
Billig, M.   103
black humour. *See* dark humour
bomolochoi (buffoon)   76, 77
Booth, W. C.   95–6, 141
Bousfield, D.   83
Bray, J.   110

bridges   23, 137
Bridget Jones's Diary (Fielding)   120, 122, 125
British National Corpus   30
Brock, T. C.   92
Brown, P.   83
Bryant, J.   41

callback   138
Cantor, J. R.   41
Catch-22 (Heller)   43, 66–8, 104–5
catharsis   19
characterization techniques   71
   disrupted interaction   100–111
   emotional engagement   71–3
   everyman/everywoman protagonist   86–93
   misfit protagonist   94–100
   social aspects of humour   73–4
   stabilizing cues   74–85
character liking   72
clowns   102–4
cognitive and affective aspects, of reading   15
   literary narrative experience and emotion   17–19
   world-based approaches to discourse comprehension   15–17
cognitive expectation   35
cognitive synergy   45
combs   23
comedy, as an expression of horror   66
comedy, granting protection from embarrassment   102–5
comedy of eccentricity   81
comicality, intention of   32
comic events   115, 119, 120, 132

Index

comic protagonist
  as 'one of us' 87–90
  perceived closeness of 90–2
  as self-deprecator 93
comic surprise 13, 134, 138, 142–3
comic suspense 13, 129–33, 138, 142
complex humorous response 9, 48, 64, 106, 111
contextual frame 16–17
contextual monitoring 17
cringe comedy. *See* cringe humour
cringe humour 12, 105–11, 147
cues 5. *See also individual entries*
  destabilizing (*see* destabilizing cues)
  stabilizing (*see* stabilizing cues)
  stylistic 5, 6, 7, 9, 13, 27, 145
Culpeper, J. 71, 84–5
Curb Your Enthusiasm (HBO sitcom) 106

Dancygier, B. 91
dark elements 49–50, 51, 59–61, 64, 68
dark humour 12, 56
  as exaggerated incongruity 60–1
  as exaggeration of dark 59–60
  as incongruity between dark and light 57–9
David, L. 106
Davis, M. H. 101, 107
decentering 18
deprecation 45–6, 49, 53. *See also* self-deprecation
destabilizing cues 7, 9, 47–51, 85
  everyman/everywoman protagonist 86–93
  humorous and non-humorous blending 61–8
  humorous mood enhancing 56–61
  knowledge degrees manipulation 133–43
  misfit protagonist 94–100

plot involvement enhancement 126–33
  protagonists in disrupted interaction 100–11
  switching to non-humorous mood 51–6
disaffiliative humour 85
discoursal point of view 29
discourse world 17, 52
disparagement humour 20, 74, 93
disposition theory, of humour 74
distance/distancing 6, 42–5, 60, 67, 98
  and immersion 6–9
  types of 29, 65
Double, O. 35
downgrading 42, 45–7, 49
downplaying 46–7
dramatic irony 133–6, 139, 140, 141
dramatic roles 76
Dynel, M. 32, 85

ego-viewpoint 91
eiron (self-deprecator) 76, 77. *See also* self-deprecation
embodiment 18
Emmott, C. 16, 17, 18, 88, 131
emotion 1, 3–4, 6–9, 13, 15, 20–1, 26, 71, 111–13, 145–7, 151
  approaches to, evoked by people in narratives 71–3
everyman/everywoman protagonist 86–93
  and literary narrative experience 17–19
  misfit protagonist 94–100
  modes and moods 27–8, 30, 33, 34, 39–41, 45, 47–51, 56, 62–6, 68–9
  plot structures 113–15
  protagonists in disrupted interaction 100–11
  story structures 121, 126, 128, 129, 143

emotion markers   30
empathy   101, 110, 112
    narrative   107–8
    and sympathy, comparison
        of   72–3
entertaining impoliteness   84–5
Ermida, I.   23, 116, 137
everyman/everywoman
    protagonist   86–93, 98, 108
excitation transfer   41
experientiality   18
experimental studies   11
exposition   114

face-threatening acts (FTAs)   83–4
faith   35
fictional worlds   16
Fielding, H.   37, 120
first-person perspective   91
focalization, linguistic manipulations
    of   110
foregrounding   42–3, 54
foreshadowing   117–18
formulate   25
Four Weddings and a Funeral (film)
    118
frame recall   131
frame switch   131
free indirect speech (FIS)   139–40
free indirect thought (FIT)   109–10
Freud, S.   20–1, 74
Frye, N.   76, 77, 86, 125

gag   115, 119, 120, 132–3, 138
gallows humour. *See* dark humour
Gavins, J.   10, 11
General Theory of Verbal Humor
    (GTVH)   22
generic humorous expansion   25
genre blends   30, 62
genre microscripts   30
Gerrig, R. J.   17–18, 114, 126, 127,
    128
Gervais, R.   106

Gray, F.   81, 104
Green, M. C.   92

Haddon, M.   3, 48, 106, 109
Heller, J.   43, 66, 104, 105
'high culture' texts   19
High Fidelity (Hornby)   77–9, 81–2,
    86–9, 93, 125, 126
Hitchhiker's Guide to the Galaxy
    (Adams)   64, 122–3, 128–9
Hobbes, T.   20, 73
Hoey, M.   114, 121, 122
hopes and preferences   127
Hornby, N.   36, 77, 95
Horton, D.   92
hot cognition   18
humorous complication   13, 119–23,
    126, 127, 132
humorous expansion   25
humorous framing   32
humorous mode   12, 31–5, 37, 38,
    41, 42, 45, 48, 53, 56, 69, 124,
    146
humorous mood   12, 33, 34, 40, 41,
    52, 53, 56–62, 69
humorous resolution   13, 119,
    121–4, 132, 143
humorous worlds, experiencing
    4–6
humour enhancers   24, 32, 116
humour studies   19
    linguistic approaches to
        humour   21–5
    schools of thought   19–21

identification and empathy   72
identification classes   90
immersion   3
    and distance   6–9
In Bruges (film)   63–4
incongruity   7–8, 21, 31, 35, 46, 63,
    82, 99, 115, 124
    internal   24, 58, 60, 67
incongruity theories   21

interactional humorous
    expansion   25
intertextuality   115
ironic distance   140
irony   38, 63
    dramatic   133–6, 139, 140, 141

jab lines   23, 24, 116
Jerome, J. K.   34, 139
'Jesus Shaves' (Sedaris)   57
jokes   5
    canned   39, 58
    non-tendentious   74
    semantic theory of   22
    tendentious   74

Keen, S.   73
King, G.   31, 62, 63, 129, 134, 138
knowledge resources (KR)   22, 23
Krutnik, F.   115, 119, 129, 132

La Fave, L.   90
Larkin Galiñanes, C.   24–5
'Learning Curve, The' (Sedaris)   45–6, 108, 130
Lee, S.   41, 54, 58–9, 103, 138
Leech, G.   29, 84, 140
Levinson, S. C.   83
Lewycka, M.   46–7, 54
linguistic humorous expansion   25
'list of three' device   58–9
literary absurd   10
literary narrative experience and emotion   17–19
locative formula   25
Lucky Jim (Amis)   24, 108
Lynn, J.   126, 133

main narrative space   91
Martin, R.   7, 32
Merchant, S.   106
meta-communication   32
metafictional distance   43–4

'Me Talk Pretty One Day' (Sedaris)   61, 97
Miall, D. S.   19, 28
Milligan, S.   37–8, 40, 41, 55, 102, 103, 104, 107
mindreading   72
minimal departure principle   16
miscommunication   81, 82, 83, 136, 147
misfit   12, 77–81, 84, 86, 102–5, 141
    protagonist as   94–100
    prototypical   80, 103
mode. *See also* humorous mode
    humour studies approaches to   31–3
    versus mood   33–6
Montoro, R.   50
mood-cue approach to filmic emotion   30
moods   27–8. *See also* humorous mood
    balance of   62
    in literary and film studies   29–30
    psychology of   28
Morreall, J.   31
Mulkay, M.   31

narcissism   37, 94–8, 100, 105, 141
narrative comedy, features of   2
narrative humour, linguistic approaches to   23–5
narratives, experiencing   18
narrative world   17–18
Nash, W.   25, 59, 137
naturalistic studies   11
Neale, S.   115, 119, 129, 132
negative preferences   126
New Comedy   125
nonsense humour   21

Office, The (BBC)   106
ordinary and unusual, blending of   99–100

parallelism 43
parasocial interaction (PSI) 92
paratelic mode 42, 44
paratelic state 31
paratexts 36–9, 48
participatory responses (p-responses) 114, 126–7
'permission to laugh' 54
play frame 32
play mode 31
positive affective schemas 50–1
positive face 83
positive impoliteness output strategies 83
positive preferences 126
possible worlds 16
preview statements 115, 118
primary mood 62
Principle of Cooperation 23
Principle of Hierarchy 23
Principle of Informativeness 23
Principle of Opposition 23
Problem-Solution pattern 121
Propp, V. 76
psychical expenditure 20
punch line 58–60, 111, 132, 136
puns 5, 25

Raskin, V. 21–2
recentering 18
recurrence 115–16, 137–43
reflexivity 63
release theories 20
relevance theory 24
replotting 127
resonance 30
reversal theory 42, 45
reversal theory approach, to humour 31
Rhetorical Processing Framework (Sanford and Emmott) 18
Right Ho, Jeeves (Wodehouse) 44, 108, 134–7
role taking 107, 108

root joke 25, 137
running gag 115, 138

Sanford, A. J. 18, 88
schema theory 50
Schopenhauer, A. 21
secondary mood 62
secret communion 96–7, 140
Secret Diary of Adrian Mole, Aged 13¾, The (Townsend) 34, 75, 95–7
Sedaris, D. 45, 57, 61, 97–100, 108, 130
self-deprecation 45–6, 86–7, 93, 94, 97–9
semantic script 22
Semantic Script Theory of Humor (SSTH) 22
Semino, E. 50
shared stereotypes 32
shared suspense 131
Short, M. 29, 140
Short History of Tractors in Ukrainian (Lewycka) 46–7, 51–3, 62, 117, 118
'Smart Guy' (Sedaris) 97–9
Smith, G. M. 30, 31, 62
Smith, S. 131
social schemata 72
Spencer, H. 20, 21
Spot of Bother, A (Haddon) 3–4, 9, 48, 57, 106, 108, 109, 111
stabilizing cues 6, 7, 33, 116–17
  complications and amusing problems generation 119–24
  foreshadowing 117–18
  humorous interactions 81–5
  humorous roles 76–81
  humorous stereotypes 74–6
  mode versus mood 33–6
  openings 39–47
  paratexts 36–9
  resolution 125–6

standards, rules and goals (SRGs) 103
stand-up comedy 138
Stockwell, P. 29, 72, 80, 89
story structures, reacting to 113.
　See also destabilizing cues
　humour studies approaches to comic plot 115–16
　plot structures, emotion, and expectation 113–15
　stabilizing cues 116–26
story-viewpoint space 91
strands 23, 137
structural parallelism 123
sub-world 55–6
Suls, J. M. 122
superiority theories 20, 24, 74
surprise, notion of 120–1, 132–3
suspense 127–9, 136
　comic 13, 129–33, 138, 142
Swann, J. 11
sympathy and empathy, comparison of 72–3

text-specific knowledge 17
textual attractors 80
text world 17, 51, 55
third person narration 91

Three Men in a Boat (Jerome) 34–5, 36, 139, 141, 143
tone, notion of 29–30
tonic states 28
Townsend, S. 34, 75
transportation 18
Triezenberg, K. E. 24, 32, 116, 137
Tsur, R. 56, 58

unreliable narration 141
unreliable narrator 95

Vandelanotte, L. 43
van Dijk, T. A. 50
van Peer, W. 43
verbal aggression 84–5
Vermeule, B. 110

Werth, P. 17
witty compression 25
Wodehouse, P. G. 44, 134, 137
Wohl, R. R. 92
Woodward, S. 107
world-based approaches, to discourse comprehension 15–17
world-switches 51
Wright, B. 109

Zillmann, D. 41

www.ingramcontent.com/pod-product-compliance
Lightning Source LLC
Chambersburg PA
CBHW052047300426
44117CB00012B/2016